OCT 2 4 2012

City of the Big Shoulders

CITY OF THE BIG SHOULDERS

An Anthology of Chicago Poetry

EDITED BY RYAN G. VAN CLEAVE

University of Iowa Press | Iowa City

University of Iowa Press, Iowa City 52242
Copyright © 2012 by the University of Iowa Press
www.uiowapress.org
Printed in the United States of America

Design by April Leidig-Higgins

The University of Iowa Press is a member of Green Press
Initiative and is committed to preserving natural resources.

Printed on acid-free paper

Library of Congress Cataloging-in-Publication Data
City of the big shoulders: an anthology of Chicago poetry /
edited by Ryan G. Van Cleave.
    p. cm.
Includes bibliographical references and index.
ISBN-13: 978-1-60938-090-8 (pbk)
ISBN-10: 1-60938-090-8 (pbk)
1. American poetry — Illinois — Chicago. 2. Chicago
(Ill.) — Poetry. I. Van Cleave, Ryan G., 1972–
PS572.C5C58 2012
811.008'035877311 — dc23   2011039539

Contents

Acknowledgments

THIS BOOK COULD NOT exist without the energy and enthusiasm of Holly Carver. Special thanks, too, to the University of Iowa Press team: Catherine Cocks, Karen Copp, James McCoy, Allison Means, Joseph Parsons, Faye Schillig, and Charlotte Wright. These are good people who live for good books. For all that they do, I am eternally grateful.

Editor's Note

AT FIRST GLANCE, it might look as if I'm the wrong person to edit this book. I was born in Neenah, Wisconsin. I don't live in Chicago now. I haven't lived in Chicago for more than a decade. I've been teaching fiction fairly exclusively for the past few years at a variety of schools. I'm sometimes considered a southern writer. I don't have much of a midwestern accent. I'm not in love with Peter Cetera's music. I've seen *The Blues Brothers* only once. I was never a fan of William "The Refrigerator" Perry. I wouldn't have guessed that Kanye West was a Chi-town native were I to use every lifeline on *Who Wants to Be a Millionaire*.

But I grew up in and around Chicago from age eleven to twenty-three—my truly formative years as a person and as a writer. I'm a die-hard Bulls and Bears fan. My family still lives in Chicago. My wife's family still lives in Chicago. I take every opportunity to visit the Windy City. I check ESPN Chicago daily. I watch WGN religiously. I secretly love Bozo, Gino's East pizza, and the swan paddleboats at the Lincoln Park lagoon. And Chicago emerges as the backdrop of many of my poems, stories, and essays. What I've come to realize is that I can easily define myself as an urban poet, a particular breed of writer who values fast-paced wit, the sublime combination of stress and surrender, the twisting agony of self-scrutinization, and the well-placed linguistic zinger. And I'm not just an urban poet in general—I'm a Chicago urban poet. It's my home base. My touchstone. My muse.

The reason I know I'm the right one to bring this project to fruition? When the idea for this book struck me, I realized it was one of the first anthologies I've done that resonated with me on a stunningly deep level. It felt as if every poem—I mean all fifteen hundred plus of them that flooded in—spoke directly to my DNA. Through its lore, its inhabitants, its physical space, its joys and sorrows, its pride and shame, all of the collected poems took their materials and inspiration from the city itself in a way that impressed me. Through these poems, I tasted Chicago again. I heard Chicago again. I praised and cursed Chicago again. And every minute of the experience was pure contentment.

Let me clarify—my relationship with Chicago is that of both insider and outsider. I love Chicago's "Da Bears" swagger. I love the deep dish pizza, the lake effect snow, the insanity of hope all Cubs fans have. I love the bustle of O'Hare. I love *ER*. I love Soldier Field, the Shedd Aquarium, and McCormick Place.

But I'm not at all like those parents who, despite overwhelming evidence to the contrary, insist their offspring is gifted. I see Chicago for its beauty and its mystery, its vibrancy and its depravity, its joy and its strangeness. There are places in this city that are simply unsafe, unclean, and unkind. There are places that are torn down, rebuilt, then torn down again in a constant state of flux.

This gathering of poems faithfully represents all this from a variety of viewpoints, styles, perspectives, and voices. They mirror the city's cosmopolitan nature well.

: : :

The University of Iowa Press prefers its poetry anthologies arranged alphabetically by authors' names, a practice begun in 2001 when Virgil Suárez and I published *Like Thunder: Poets Respond to Violence in America*. We didn't want to have to try to make sections according to some arbitrary themes. "These poems are about sexual violence," "these are about domestic violence," etc. And with this anthology, I similarly don't want to draw such artificial, limiting distinctions. Even in poems that appear to be fairly straightforward in their topics, such as Adrian Matejka's "Jack Johnson Comes to Chicago," Lola Haskins's "Dearborn North Apartments," and Ellen Wehle's "Cloud Gate," the poems still range across a host of themes and topics. So I agree—an alphabetical arrangement is the best way for them to find their own voices and create unexpected bursts of melody, as does Brenda Yates's encompassing "Chicago," which follows Stephen Caldwell Wright's "Chicago Chronicle," or Maya Quintero's curiously angry "Second Sister Terrorizes Second City" coming before Teresa Scollon's soft, luxurious poem, "Pigeon Lady." Unfettered by subjective groupings of "theme" or "aesthetic," these poems refuse an easy, narrow definition of what makes Chicago *Chicago*.

I'm also extraordinarily pleased by the unexpected avenues from which some of these poems have arrived. Todd James Pierce, primarily known as a novelist and the winner of the 2006 Drue Heinz Prize for short fiction, shares a lovely, well-researched poem about Walt Disney in the late 1940s entitled "Tracks on the Ground, Tracks in the Sky." A humorous baseball poem, "Hibernation," comes not from a Wrigleyville native but from Bart Edelman, a California baseball fan with some sympathy for the luckless Cubbies. And there's Jarret Keene—a Tampa-born son of a firefighter, who now works for a big casino in Vegas (the source of the "corporate enslavement" where he's "chained to [his] cubicle," I suspect)—who offers a compelling epistolary poem to Steve Albini, the founder and owner of a Chicago recording studio, Electrical Audio. Albini's also known as a member of the bands Big Black, Rapeman, Flour, and Shellac.

Plus there's a host of slam/spoken word poets whose work rarely finds its way into traditional print anthologies. Me? I'm delighted to have them represent Chi-town, considered by many to be the home of slam poetry.

Like Chicago itself, the pleasures this grouping of poems offers may vary by taste. A few writers responded to my Call for Submissions and said, "You HAVE to include a poem about _____" (fill in that blank with any of a hundred Chicago-related people, places, and things). For every five Chicago icons mentioned in this book, there's probably another some reader feels is a lamentable oversight. It's nearly impossible to give a comprehensive taking-stock of any single place in an individual book, though with the diverse manifestations of these particular poems, I believe we get at some of the core truths of the multi-faceted urban environment so many of us have grown to love. Through the combined efforts of all of these poems, perhaps we can help decipher a bit of the complex appeal that is Second City, City by the Lake, New Gotham, Paris on the Prairie, and the Heart of America.

: : :

1916's *The Chicago Anthology: A Collection of Verse from the Work of Chicago Poets,* edited by Charles G. Blanden and Minna Mathison, was one of the first attempts to define and present the poetry of Chicago as a distinctive, unified body of literature. Indeed, plenty of writers have gone on to be defined by their relationship to this city: Carl Sandburg, Karl Shapiro, George Dillon, Edgar Lee Masters, and Gwendolyn Brooks, to name just a few. And this anthology takes up the literary torch with some of America's brightest poetic lights who've been touched by Chicago's many inspirations. But by no means is the poetic conversation about Chicago over. It's a vital, important part of the literary landscape of America, and it's clear that new members are appearing daily. More than a few contributors remarked in their cover letters that the literature of Chicago is experiencing a renaissance. After seeing so many fine new writers and quality veterans, I'm inclined to agree.

The poems in this anthology are not just beautiful objects to be enjoyed once and then put away. Savor the ones that seem written specifically for you. Consider the rest a challenge to be met. I guarantee at least three poems in this book will unlock a memory (real or imagined) of State Street vendor brats, the cacophony of smells that is the Taste of Chicago, or the sight of children skating at dusk at Daley Plaza—even if you've never been to the Windy City itself yet.

Chicago is my hometown. No matter your background or interests, these poems do a fine job of making it yours, too.

City of the Big Shoulders

Routes

KATHRYN ALMY

The glaciers came down from Wisconsin
and carved Illinois into moraines and ravines
and 10,000 years later—after the pioneers, Al Capone,
and the Manhattan Project—my parents
led us in to a small patch of wild inside
the suburbs. Every weekend for fourteen years
we trooped out to walk the dog and we didn't stop
even after she died. We picked wild strawberries
in June, sledded down the bank onto the frozen lake,
and explored smoke-blackened picnic shelters
and trails whose look and length
changed as I aged. The trails led us out
into the world—couples making out
along the trail, Gay Pride spray-painted
on the stone bridge, people who hit their dogs
or children. I found a pornographic photo
in the strawberry field and hid it
on a high shelf in our bathroom. Later
we ranged further out to wilder places
with less litter and riffraff, where we knelt
in poison ivy, picked—and ate—puffball mushrooms
the size of human skulls, found a duck tangled
in fishing line and six-pack rings, cut a snake
out of a beer can. Nobody said anything,
but we were different from the families at the picnic
grounds whose old people didn't speak English,
different from the hippies and the men who backed their cars
into the lot and followed each other into the bushes.
My parents led us single file
on the deer paths and along old roads
paved with broken glass. I walked inside
my own escape set against weedy prairies, gray
winter oaks—all the dusty city nature, lost
under the enormous space above my head.

At the Crawford Coal-Fired Power Plant

NIN ANDREWS

As she inhales the scent of boiled eggs, the woman thinks of childhood, the farm she grew up on, the chicken coop down the hill from the clothesline. She thinks how back then, coal dust could coat sheets in a matter of minutes. Not anymore. These days it's what she can't see that worries her. But the plant manager says that this is a forward-thinking plant. *Why? Because Crawford has reduced its mercury emissions ahead of schedule. And its nitrogen oxide emissions are down 30%.* She doesn't ask him what schedule. She doesn't ask how much mercury or nitrogen oxide a person should breathe. Nor does she ask why the plant has been in the news in the past few years for spewing deadly toxins into the Chicago air and increasing the risk and incidence rate of asthma. She's a guest here, so she smiles and nods when he hands her a hardhat, goggles, and orange earplugs. The building hums and throbs around them. She can barely make out his words as he shouts and points. She sees the pulverizer where the coal is crushed and blown into a furnace. She sees the boiler, the precipitator, and the fireball that glows like a small sun. In one room fly ash lands on her black sweater. She tries to brush it off, but it sticks to the cashmere. She asks if she should wear a facemask. She asks if the ash is dangerous. *No, no,* he says. *These days we collect the ash from the precipitator and gather it into bins. Then we sell it for cement.* But it's in the air, she tries to tell him, pointing to the ash she sees rising like dust. She's not sure he hears her. She's not sure he sees what she means. He keeps opening and closing his mouth, as if to reassure her, as if to explain that everything is fine. She has nothing to worry about here.

Time Travel

DORI APPEL

Invading her privacy was easy.
An internet click and there it was:
Michelle Obama's childhood home
on Euclid Avenue, dark Chicago brick
like the ones surrounding it.

Passing it daily as I rushed
to school (while avoiding
a certain brindle dog),
I probably never really
looked at it. To think

that she wasn't even born yet,
and by the time she'd arrived
the dog was long dead and
the neighborhood was struggling
with a classic color change. By then,

fluorescent lights had probably
replaced the heavy hanging globes
at Bryn Mawr Elementary,
though I doubt they relieved
its gloominess. To think

that her steps echoed mine
from first grade to eighth—
turning off Euclid to 74th,
then speeding up faster on
the last block to Jeffrey,

while my own young daughter,
who is exactly her age,
was nearing her school with
her hand in mine, on a street
a world away.

Chicago Deep Dish

CRISTIN O'KEEFE APTOWICZ

Oh, your pizzas. Your epic, molten pizzas.
Your thick, spitting, spectacular sausages,
the breakfasts you eat right out of the skillet.

Oh, Chicago, when I think of you, I rub
the phantom grease off my chin and moan.
Your food is shudderingly shameless.

Here in Gotham, we've got a lot, but
you know what? You can't buy Old Style
in New York City, or Garrett's popcorn,

you can't watch grown men eat pickles
with peppermint sticks screwed into 'em,
or get an Italian Beef after the ballgame.

Your sandwiches are the monuments
to excess our skyscrapers try to be.
Your sweet teas, impossibly sweeter.

Chicago, you make me want to hide
my city's waifish media-friendly chefs,
their cashmere scarves and *emulsions*.

No, I want to tell them, give me Chicago.
Give me meats covered in bubbling cheeses,
dough covered in cream and sugar, give me

a cup of coffee so strong the mug trembles.
I don't want your trendy, or your avant-garde.
I want Chicago, deep dish. I want to eat

in a city smart enough to know that if you
are going to have that heart attack, you might
as well as have the pleasure of knowing

you've really earned it.

Chicago's Monuments

RANE ARROYO

I lived in a city protected from pared winds
     by stoic statues of
naked war heroes, abstract peacocks, and
     unknown citizens.
They were too heavy, collectively, for forces
     of nature or man
to move my city into another time zone or
     foreign myths.
Lies in our own images kept us feeling safe,
     but I once cried for
a lost love under a stone Columbus, enjoying
     the pretend danger.
Statues, like "Aesthetics," weren't shy or too
     ashamed to be
anatomically correct for we're proud not to be
     figleaf moralists.
Let's see if when cockroaches outsurvive
     humans—the unspeakable
said aloud—if their bug statues remain
     true-to-size and
don't trumpet their moral superiority.

Hancock O'Hare

MICHAEL AUSTIN

When I was a boy my sister took me
to the top of the John Hancock
where I pushed my chin out
past my knuckles on a railing
to see the little cars on the street below

I flew a lot in those days
and when we took off from O'Hare
I watched vehicles and buildings shrink
until they looked like toys and then lost their shape

I tried to imagine the moment
of takeoff
or landing
when cars looked just like they
did from the Hancock

I have not seen a car from up there in years

I go up and look out
at other buildings now
and airplanes
coming and going
above the backlit horizon

I still look out from airplanes
on takeoff
and landing
watching cars and houses fall away like tiny models
or fade up into actual size

From the Hancock
when I see those planes
going up or down
by O'Hare

I wonder who is looking at what in them
and whether they can see
the tall black building on the lakefront
next to Oak Street Beach
that tiny, sooty toothpick stuck in the sand

Yes, We Can

MARVIN BELL

*On the inauguration of Barack Obama as the 44th president
of the United States of America, Jan. 20, 2009*

We are a people who began from a Yes,
A nation born of the yes in the farmland,
The yes engraved in the dirt and stone,
In the mines, in the sea, in the machines
That made girders that made cities,
In the big ideas that make us human,
In the yes that comes to every street
Where there endures a love of forebears
And a net for children when they fall,
Where there was a yes to "Let's try,"
And a yes, we can do better, and a yes
That grew to enfold our largest America.
Yes to the high-rise ironworker, yes
To the diggers of tunnels and the pilots,
Yes to those still on line, to the makers,
The builders, the haulers, the guardians,
To the teachers who had to make do.
It is the yes that sings, and lights up the dark.
It is the yes in the myriad colors of unity,
And in what it means to be a grownup.
In the gasoline rainbows by the curb
As the parent takes his child to school
And the parent takes her lunch bucket to work,
And the father carries his papers
And the schoolchild her homework,
The carpenter her measure, the fisherman his tackle,
And who dares say, no we can't, at sunup?
Have you heard the cry of yes in the newborn
At his mother's breast, and heard the yes
Whispering in the fields at harvest time?
There is a yes that will not be shushed
In the head of the scientist weary at her desk
And in the doctor as he studies the X-rays

After hours. We are the yes from every continent,
The yes born of flesh and blood that came
By steerage and slave ship, the manyness
Of all who were this nation's first people
Or came after, by many paths, whatever it took.
We have been an aggregate of wishes
And hopes, of the future, of blessings, of aches
And pleasure, of the sacred liberties
For which families have labored and grieved.
We still want to say yes, yes to equality,
Yes to the best in us, yes and yes to the idea
That we will be judged by what we do for others
For free, and so we have said yes, and yes again,
One nation, one people, and yes, we can.

Ted Stone Morning

MARY GRACE BERTULFO

Home, prairie-muck dried
onto the seams of my field pants,
hiking boots splattered with mud,
hair in pleasant disarray.
The scent of freedom
still clings to me.
Just an hour before,
by watch-time, by analog hands,
I walked amidst the shaking
dry winter sedges
of the Ted Stone Preserve.

Rare prairie lands
14,000 years in the making,
a glacier's passing,
strewn dolomite and limestone,
crumbling soft-edged rocks,
and the whimsy of a universe
where terrains stretch, wrinkle,
move in slow motion.
Quick-footed Barbara Birmingham,
summer silver hair,
storm seasoned,
gives me *her* tour.
It's a steward's rambling hike
through prairie, grove, and savanna
she's nurtured for 14 years,
another gift of time.

I follow her silhouette,
pick out the faint trail,
squish, slide upon dense mud.
Below, thirsty fibrous roots
push through soil deep as a woman.
Above, a vista of thin, tufted stalks,

sprays of feathery beige and shifting grays
sway and rattle in the wind.
It is the hidden Chicago wilderness,
our natural heritage,
studded and tucked between
lamp-posted neighborhoods,
brick and strip-malled burbs,
and ribbons of concrete.
With each kiss of mud,
my body breathes a question:
By now, don't we know
all wild places are God's first?

Barbara leans in close, points,
issues a warm-throated chuckle
as if we're two women in cahoots.
Sly humor lines her cheeks.
There are secrets at her fingertips—
gray praying mantis cocoon,
pasture rose topped by
a berry-looking ovary,
little blue stem grass drooping
heavy with seeds,
sacred ground
where Barbara made sure I saw
how females recreate nature,
how life goes on
through our tenacity.

Postcard from Buddy Guy's Legends: Bar and Grill, Chicago

ALLEN BRADEN

Order the Big Bayou Blue Plate Special. Here, their motto could be the city's. "Damn Right We've Got the Blues!" The song I do for you more than music, color, clinical depression, more than beach glass blue; Picasso blue; Fourth of July bottle rocket burst blue; low-rise blue of distressed denim blue revealing a field guide to *Electric Blue* on some Betty's hipbone in tattooed blue; through her lips, clouds of nicotine blue; CPD Kevlar blue; The Blue Men blue; Bears and Cubs fanatics embroidered blue (or worse yet there's those game day, let's-git-a-lil-bit-rowdy, face-painted blues); pool cue chalk blue; Bar-B-Que brick blue; this quick flicker of floozy synthetic blue in a back alley off of Wabash Avenue where a busboy practices fly casting, pretending he's somewhere else, some place marvelously new.

Yours truly,
Allen

I Saw You

JOHN BRADLEY

Where: Wilton Ave. The algebra of your nameless blond hair. I think you went offline, which made you flutter, then disappear.

Where: Weiner's Circle. You favor green or red South American scarves. I wear useless knowledge. Save my village.

Where: Sears at North Riverside. We talked about trying to find a pair of jeans for your full lips. You have a tiny mole that wore a polo shirt, if you remember.

Where: Chase ATM Milwaukee and Ashland. We noticed an angel with greasy wings teleported away. I had gotten so lost on the cell phone, my face ended up behind me.

Where: O'Hare Transit to Remote Parking. I was drunk on sushi. My name was something like Ian. In the parking lot, Sunday afternoon slowly drove away.

Where: Red Eyes Coffee Shop. You wear blue jackets that aren't warm enough. I wear warm jackets that aren't blue enough.

Where: The Two Way Lounge. One text texting another. Not much proper grammar there, so you should know who you are.

Where: Rogers Park Walgreens. I was wandering the aisles in search of Lemonheads. You were wearing a shirt that said something like "No Shit, Chicago."

Where: CTA Red Line Car 2663. You told me after you finish the Peace Corps, it's Roller Derby. By the way, I have your eyelashes, if you remember, dork.

The Last Fortune Teller of Chicago

JOHN F. BUCKLEY AND MARTIN OTT

His great-grandfather was a one-legged sausage grinder
who put a hundred year curse on the Cubs after the brawl
which left him hobbled—his dark gift for his pickled brats,
the favorite of pregnant women, gangsters and card runners.

His grandfather cast chimeric statues, heads and broad
shoulders of giant bulls atop pork bellies, with clay geese feet
and wild-onion tails. He drowned in the lake, having leapt from
the El on the defunct Gray Line running east to the water.

He had two fathers—one who gunned his Chrysler Le Baron
across an ice bridge through bum encampments, hidden hatches
smelling of baby powder; his second father dancing an Irish jig
blindfolded on skyscraper girders, a twin magic of disappearance.

One or more of them gave his mother a phantom pregnancy,
his dry older sister who never came forth from the womb,
anti-Lazarus, who knocked around until he arrived, stitching
his caul to his face. He was born blue and embroidered, gasping

like carp in the birth canal of the Chicago River, churned green
for the first time with the dumping of fluoroscein. The doctor
who slapped him learned the language of love and sired hump
shouldered boys, future eyes and ears for unerring prophecies.

And all around the last fortune teller, the skin on his sockets
like the soles of his feet, came traveling visions, sights of boxcars
and carnival destinies, hobo clowns carving up fates in stockyards.
He pushed a broom at the stock exchange, shoving rent tickets

into a bag that he used to build scarecrows promising perfect
crops to the farmers that paid him homage. Rain never touched
his downed squid of a face, and the women who sat on his crystal
ball found men, marriage and children that smelled like kielbasa.

Sixteen

MELISA CAHNMANN-TAYLOR

Honeybee in Greek,
he said. My name slurred
from a shotglass of ouzo

balanced on his head. Fed my first
dolma, I wished to be rolled
and eaten with my giggling

high school friends.
Mé-lisa like he was smelling me,
danced around the room, slapping

one knee, calling me to rocks,
his Adriatic Sea like some nymph
with new breasts tied to stones.

Weekends we dressed like twinkled
buildings, left the burbs
with a borrowed car for

Greektown and Oldtown,
shouting our names
through back alleys, suckling

around the groan and tail
of older men. We were
going somewhere, sure of it,

as we heard our names drop
like exotic cities
from hypnotic mouths.

Everything Is

KAREN CARCIA

unlike the field
      I look out upon
from my barred window.

A city landscape of flat
      black roofs and side
alleys always speaks

volumes about plains
      that never end. These
small birds come

to my window remind
      me why it is almost
better to live one place

and long for another.
      Some days we think
the world is like us:

small, forgettable. So,
      we search for reminders
and a man misses brown

so much he imports
      sparrows
from England. Because

nothing's really like rain
      except rain. But

whatever river we've diverted
      will find its way back
to us. Lost on the corner of

Clark and Foster—suddenly
       birds. Just who
thought *that* sound should

signify to the blind, to us
       walk now,
it's okay to walk.

Jean Baptiste

JAMES E. CHERRY

I don't know nothing 'bout no Chicago.
When I got there wasn't nothing but swamp
land the white folks didn't want.
But I made best out of what I had setting traps
for martens like I learned from Choctaw
doing business with folk as far away as Canada
making friends with the Indians and helping
them settle they affairs and 'fore long, I had
a mill, bakery, dairy, stables, house of five rooms
with expensive furniture and fine art to look at
the kind they have in France where father sent me
 to study after mama was killed on Saint-Dominique.

At that Catholic school, I learned all the Spanish
and English I needed, so Clamorgan and I let out
for the new world of New Orleans where Choctaw
was working at a Catholic Mission until the three
of us trailed the Mississip to Peoria. There I became
Black Chief among the Potawatomi where the eagle
was my sign, married Kittahawa and we had a son
a daughter and 800 acres of land. I was 25 years old.

After that, that's when I came north to this here place
on the western shore of the lake, the place the Indians
call Eschikagow because it smelled so bad and like I
said things were going real well until war broke out,
my wife and son died and I sold the land and moved
with my daughter Suzanne, named after my mother,
to Saint Louie.

Things change like that. They either change
to a new beginning or change to a new ending.
But they bound to change. I know that for a fact.
But I don't know nothing 'bout no Chicago.

Sleeping with Carl

SUSAN DEER CLOUD

(. . . *Pocahontas' body, lovely as a poplar, sweet as a red haw
in November or a pawpaw in May, did she wonder?*)

I can't even recall where I stumbled upon
Caedmon Records. But at fourteen
I sent for Carl Sandburg reading
his poems on Caedmon 78 LP . . .
paid for it with babysitting money.

And what did I know of Chicago,
skyscrapers and hog butchers?
A girl much like Pocahontas,
I lived in 1960s Catskills
and kept my own poetry secret.

I had seen photographs of Sandburg,
thought his star-white hair beautiful
and loved his face whose skin
I imagined would feel intricate
as the fossils I collected.

Every night I let the black record
fall down the spindle of my small
red record player, let my virgin body
fall into my little bed while Carl
began speaking his poetry

into my mountain bedroom.
Carl, he spoke the language of Indians,
soft, deep, slow and of root-thick earth
with its music of rivers. Indian-named
Chicago never took that from him.

I wore a flimsy peignoir that May
Carl first came to my room. So much

I've forgotten, yet in my November
I recall the gown was spring green
and filmy as dream.

I held a pillow to me as if it
were a man's body seeking mine,
while moonlight straddled
my wondering hands, legs, mouth . . .
Carl, first poet I slept with.

Hotel Dana

JAMES CONROY

State and Erie, 2006

A wrecking ball came to the rancid flophouse
on State and Erie. Condo moguls cheered
and City planners saluted each other with
lunch at Gibson's Steakhouse.
Heaped with brick and metal are crack vials
and much-shared, used syringes, and empty
screw-top bottles of worse than rot-gut.
River North neighbors cheer: no more drunks,
no addicts, no maimed, creepy-looking ghouls
to scare our children or urine alley smell and
sleeping shadows propped against open windows on
arid nights.
So an ode to the last of Dana's desperate friends.
Ex-lodgers now in ranks of the homeless
army; army of a nation all too much on its own.
When did it become a nuisance or crime
being broke or defeated by your dreams?
And mental illness spurned as anathema again?
Suppose there might be, may have been, gold
in that rubble that now isn't even scrapworthy.
From across the street I hear sounds lost to the
mortar-crack and diesel. The wail of errant souls
looking for themselves, or, if given up, clutching
a shred of peace that had four walls.
Do I hear jazz riffs, snatches of poems, the
scratching of charcoal on a torn sketchbook page?
Remember suffering for art? Before people
plagiarized to fame or exploited until it became
chic. When agents agent-ed and work
was its own publicist for free speech. When we
listened, read, thought, and viewed and
didn't refer to it as mere entertainment.
This I see in the dangling ripped pipes
and hear in the deadening lead crunches.

The passers-by shout, "Finally!
Good riddance," as they stroll on to shop.
If I can afford my addictions, that's okay.
If my craft won't buy a meal, another story.
No garret left not been swallowed up
for the prized River view. Streets are not for
living, they're for parading what we buy on good
credit. No hovel need be spared for a Bellows,
Algren, Farrell, Wright, or Sandburg to
pitch the fight of muse against their own demons.
Here it is one, maybe two towers shy of true
Eden. But you must have it all before you arrive.

Low Ride Elegy

TIMOTHY COOK

The Blood Thirsty Death Hogs
was the name of our gang.
Me, my brother, his friends
Jason, Nate, Jimmy, Matt

rode souped-up vintage
Schwinn Cruisers, made in
Chicago, with whitewall tires,
chopper handle bars, banana seats.

Matt listened to Oblivion,
the Clash, the Dead Kennedys,
wore combat boots and t-shirts
with rolled-up sleeves.

My bike was blue and white
with a train engine fender light
and hawk feather banana seat.
I called it the American Dream.

What he did with himself
when we weren't tripping
on acid or night swimming
off Foster Pier I'll never know.

Riding along Diversey Harbor
I wanted to turn my handlebars,
sink down to half-buried tires
and moss-covered shopping carts.

Campus Taxi

NINA CORWIN

The meter ticks off blocks,
one neatly groomed corner at a time.
Across the quads, tenured professors shuffle
through yellowing notes for classes taught
some thirty-odd years. Eyes hollow
with a common decay, Ph.D. students stoop
beneath weighty dissertations, a flock
of pale, earthbound angels. His own remains
unfinished. But fares here appreciate
his grasp of history, giving bigger tips
for a well-wrought phrase. He drifts past
the Medici, where undergrads linger
over pizza, past Jimmy's Tap on Garfield,
leaving the Midway, an ivory sigh
behind. He dreams that if he stays
under its shadow any longer, the ivy will swarm
over his limbs like every other campus edifice.
As it is, his Einstein flyaway hair won't
stop growing, a matter which strikes him
with mixed alarm and fascination.
It seems he has his own silver halo, something
generally accorded only the virtuous
and the dead. It grows late
and fares at this hour are hard to come by.
He doubles back to cruise the all-night library.
Behind the moon, the Mind Almighty brocades
tightly-woven minutiae into glittering insights.
In a few hours, he can return to the arms
of his books, their lengthy titles entwining
like barbed wire. His brain
is outgrowing his skull—a dense, fallen orb
of gray matter rolling downhill,
picking up leaves and twigs as it goes.

Michael Jordan

CURTIS L. CRISLER

A hot zephyr blew in from east coast,
crossing breezes with Windy City—
a dunking mad fool. Before precision fade-
aways and Cirque du Soleil awe, before
chrome dome, when he Teeny Weenie Afro,
when Sleepy Floyd passed North Carolina
championship, no one visualized it, put prayers
up, but Mike got it stuck in brain how Dr. J.
went freeze-frame from free-throw into deep
space nine, took away velcro young black boys
tear when their mothers dream them traced in
white lines, like how a new mole births
insecurity.
       His tongue hung out his mouth
like he'd bite it off—that's code for "take this
for not believing in me, those before me, dreams
to come"—jazzing some juke, a Muddy Water
Hoopla, in a zone, a greedy Komodo Dragon.
He rose, the ambient light of God, thirsty for
pious purity, took us to church again and again
and again. In honor we coined him M. Jay,
and he got all high on Spike Lee joints since
we never see two black millionaires cavort.

And what got thick in Mike was a moon full
of spirit, shining its flavor from night beams
into the darkness, in that chunky pot of wisdom:
a nod from hard father, firm pat on firm butt
from teammate, a loud smile from mama, who
taught all indifference (the ingredients) works
together: life's tricky fierce flavor, come from
a strong stank roux in the gumbo, dorsal dark
line out deveined shrimp, like ocean dark mud
atop oyster, greasy haze on meat under casing
of sausage—gut from what bubbles before so

fresh—so clean. Mike honed all street babies to
reach beyond dank, bleak, varicose concrete of
bland projections, or angry, dirty, mouths who
beat us into self hate; he got us to 5th dimension
to grab smoke-hot, flailing, tail of a marvelous.

summer news

MARY CROSS

to joseph cornell

we hoist up our living room windows   unlatch storms and screens   so the white-
crowned sparrows and goldfinches can feed on nyger seed
from our coffee table   a postcard of your soap bubble set   1948   lies face up

no bird dares to step on it

two cats prevail over the formidable velvet chair dyed
aubergine   for your mother

nobody knows how to wear out birds

we let them shuck the seed where they want   land on picture frames
use the second-floor parlor as they will   we're renters   joseph   not owners
but we still do as we please

seven city blocks away   the park district has covered 4000 trashcans with iron grids so
gulls and crows can't pick away unclaimed doritos

from 14-ounce bags   whacking against the wind
and that's why we can't swim at montrose beach

e. coli from the birds   and   stray sewage

they've hired a crew of border collies to bark
at anything that flies
as they glide along the shoreline in rowboats manned by lifeguards

some say their collars are radioactive   isotopes flattening the atmosphere
for sale at a kiosk on the pier

we are flummoxed by the 16 bags of popcorn
the size of beanbag chairs piled up on the boardwalk like a lumpy skyline

surrounded by 50-pound drums of coconut oil
not for our hair or skin but for the kernels

something for your boxes   joseph?

good fortune bracelets   an earthly scent
a glass prism   incense   a tiny elephant
figurine from a passage to india

where a korean man polishes worry stones
hands out samples of mackinac island fudge
with recyclable toothpicks

the water taxies are grounded until further notice

but that's no matter   joseph
we have everything we need right here   in front of us
amassing dust

Still Life with Zeno and File Footage

JAMES D'AGOSTINO

for Walter Payton

As much Autumn as you ever are
going to get is going to have

to be the name of this moment
forever. Everything is sadder

in the slo mo. Dead halfbacks.
Sentences. Soon it won't be so

late. Daylight Savings,
i.e., we're almost over with

October and already dead
last in the standings. This is

the season, the capitulating sugars
of the chlorophyll. All bodies

fall at 9.8 meters per second
per second and yours is only one

inside those snowstorms. Chicago.
Green Bay. Minnesota. Such a simple

wish this ever is. Such daylight
to be saved. 2 A.M. is 1 A.M.

but that gets us only halfway
there. The day it

used to be. The very day.
The 15. The 10. The 5.

Ravenswood

STUART DYBEK

Pigeons fold their wings and fade
into the gray facades of public places;
flags descend from banks, silk slips
floating to beds. Hips thrust

like those of lovers, as workers crank
through turnstiles, and waiting
for the Ravenswood express at stations
level with the sun, they shield their eyes

with newspapers against a dying radiance;
that lull between trains
when stratified fire is balanced

on a gleaming spire. Night doesn't *fall*,
but rather, all the disregarded shadows of a day
flock like blackbirds, and suddenly rise.

Hibernation

BART EDELMAN

You have to think it's simply
A matter of hibernation—
Perhaps, the longest on record,
But nothing more than that.
And the odds must slowly
Be sliding in our favor—
100 seasons waiting
For just the right year
To end this drought
And throw back our big shoulders.

The best and the brightest
Ever to play the game,
Came to wave the hickory stick,
Pitch fastballs of fire,
Fill the bleachers with any bum
You'd gladly buy a beer,
And listen to Harry
Take us out to the ballgame.

Who really knows?
Maybe it was the curse of the goat
Or simply too much illumination,
Just when darkness might have given way
To natural light that arrives
Before the end of a long sleep
And the eventual promise
October offers this windy city,
In exchange for another home run
Hit above the ivy-filled wall
With no return in sight.

Sweet Ernie would love to play two,
If given the slightest chance
To tinker forever in a Cubbies uniform.

Billy, Fergie, Gabby, Kenny, Ron, and Ryne
Only need to wake from slumber's embrace
And set the record straight—
Run the table, wire to wire—
As if 1908 were yesterday,
And we could hear
The bear roar once more.

Chicago Union Stockyards Circa 1957

SUSAN ELBE

On my block, all we knew of it was when the blow

> blew it our way, the smell of fear
> and blood, a stink that meant work

for so many. In winter, two shifts every day
six days a week, finger-whitening cold,

bone-crushing gears, the slick machinery of death.

Divided in their work as in their lives—the Irish

> ran the boardwalks, swatting flies,
> herding livestock in and out of pens.

Mexicans dried and salted lamb skins
in the rank cool of hide cellars.

The Poles and coloreds side-slipped on the killing floor.

On my block, stump-fingered, steel-toed welders

> came home swinging domed
> lunch buckets in long arcs

and soup-factory workers leaned on fences
smoking, in white rowboat hats.

A hooked moon lifted, red.

Legend has it, near the Yards, families kept canaries

> to muffle panicked cries of animals,
> their sweet trilling high against

the lowing dark, the gravity of *disassembling*.

150 Years of Chicago Architecture

DINA ELENBOGEN

In demolishing buildings
we see how they were made,
how many years of wind
and water, what they carried
inside themselves.
From the patterns in door knobs
the winding of steps,
we can guess what year it was,
what people wore, if they undressed
in the light or dark.

When you take off my clothes
you can't see my heart.
When you try to push
all the way inside
you cannot see my past—
but when you make it so I cannot breathe
or let go, you can see
with what fragile pieces I was made,
how easily I come undone.

I want to live in a house built long after the fire.
I want the old smells of rain held captive,
mildew and dust. I want a giant willow
to weep over my house in autumn,
a corner where even my bravest son
would be afraid to hide.
I want wood so solid
it can't be stripped
except to discover Jacaranda
underneath.

Cheo Saw an Angel on Division Street

MARTÍN ESPADA

Cheo was a Latin King,
but tomorrow he jumps a bus
for the winter country,
away from the city,
with a vision of the barrio
that will glow
at every gas station
along the smooth night
of the highway.

Cheo saw an angel
on Division Street today:
wandering the block
in the wrong gang colors,
condemned by a sickle of inquisitors,
baptized in gasoline,
purified with a match,
shrieking angel, burning heretic,
brilliant crucifix
thrown through a skylight
on the roof.

And when the chorus of glass
exploded in crescendo,
Cheo heard the angel say:

I am the heat that will flush your face,
I am the sweat of your skin,
I am the one you will pray for,
I am the kiss of the cross.

Loop

JOHN W. EVANS

Buildings aspire to height rather than volume,
as though the sun at any moment might stop shining
all the way down to commuters in heavy coats,

stumping the Rust Belt winter beneath elevated trains.
They look up through awnings blocking out sky as steam
from coffee cups dissolves into the in-between.

Lake-effect snow swirls; the real stuff sticks.
Wind off Lake Michigan spirals through the skyline,
finds a place to enter and leave and enter again,

bowing stop signs, glazing the corner slush,
snapping pellets against industrial windowpanes
with all the permanence of keys clacking out

notices past due. Ours is a perpetual debt
of languages, characters, gestures, implications.
The profit is collective and distributed top-down.

We wake one morning and something is different
in the reflection of a body. We verify with touch
and the secret handshake only demonstrates a consensus,

among strangers, that one kind of arriving is private,
a space between here and there that only we shall cross.

Asked for a Happy Memory of Her Father, She Recalls Wrigley Field

BETH ANN FENNELLY

His drinking was different in sunshine,
as if it couldn't be bad. Sudden, manic,
he swung into a laugh, bought me
two ice creams, said *One for each hand.*

Half the hot inning I licked Good Humor
running down wrists. My bird-mother
earlier, packing my pockets with sunblock,
had hopped her warning: *Be careful.*

So, pinned between his knees, I held
his Old Style in both hands
while he streaked the lotion on my cheeks
and slurred *My little Indian princess.*

Home run: the hairy necks of men in front
jumped up, thighs torn from gummy green bleachers
to join the violent scramble. Father
held me close and said *Be careful,*

be careful. But why should I be full of care
with his thick arm circling my shoulders,
with a high smiling sun, like a home run,
in the upper right-hand corner of the sky?

Radar Ghosts

MICHAEL FILIMOWICZ

in the zeppelin's windows the aquarium city
shows a gold onion dome unspiraling
blossoming for docking atop a new office tower
suspicious and gaudy in 1928

when travelers with visas and faith in their telescopes
sporting new lenses and shiny screws
conspired with mapmakers in the viewing lounge
to designate a continent's armpit

a little capital went a long way on the map
in each grid cell were dots, penciled names
most would never lay eyes
on the actual earth therein

which was for churning anyway, or
trawling, drilling, paving, filling, piling
the heat and the boiling begat
a foam you can walk on

in eddies under the bridges
where the city synthesizes its shadows
to combat the homely flickering glow
of ten million entertainment centers

meanwhile an arsonist's skyline effects
replays in the valley of rooftops
the black fountains of smoke and ash
fade into blue, bluer, black

where antique space-stations rustless in their orbits
bear witness to terrestrial accumulations of motion
mute holocausts of sun tuck heat into vacuum
burning antennas in 2001

when two escalator strangers smile through blue windows
hiding their heat beneath clothes which sting
there is memory in the paralysis
of a ride between two points

they cross between the gleam and the corners
that was the dream of the swamp-sellers
the escalator loops and the lovers embrace
the empty space which swells between them

With My Blue Flowered Dress

JENNIFER S. FLESCHER

You look like a farm girl,
he said. He touched the sleeve.
I know a farm. Fire
heats and cooks and wakes
the must, the oily sheep flax . . .
His black leather better

suited the cold Chicago wind.
White waves. I know.
The still spinning wheel.
Cast iron. Buttermilk.
The rain was hard, and he
was in the company

of strangers. *The farm*
girl who appears
when your car dies
in the middle of nowhere.
The kitchen. Morning.
Cold tiles, eggs still hen-warm.

The farm girl who appears.
My wooden shoes
were trashed from the rocks
that guard the city. I know.
A fireplace.
A table, broad for writing

and a bed
composed for you
in my mouth.
And then you never leave.
I stand barefoot.
I throw my shoes in.

Republic Steel Chicago South Works

RENNY GOLDEN

I

In the heat of May 1937, my grandfather
sits in the spring grass of an industrial park
with hundreds of striking steelworkers.

Boys' kites throw diamond colors to a cobalt sky,
men tilt beer barrels, pitch horseshoes onto stakes
hammered down by thick, calloused hands.

When the police circle that Memorial Day picnic, men form
lines, a sun-mottled army of white undershirts, red and black
suspenders. They move as one in front of their families.

Tension runs the line the way a bass pulls tight,
the hook tearing deeper and deeper.
The strikers wait for the circle of blue shirts to loosen.

When Captain Mooney orders the police circle to tighten
everyone bolts, a thunder of feet beat through wicker baskets,
plates of beans, sauerkraut, pig knuckles, fried chicken.

The shots split Leon Franchesco's faded work shirt,
a stain opening like a rose. Sam Popovitch, in his seventies, can't run.
He falls holding his smashed skull, his dying eyes astonished.

An accordion winces where they push Dolan from a line of shots.
Workers pull the fallen Sam Causey into someone's car
but cops drag him bleeding onto the street.

Otis Jones and nine others will not see the strike end.
Otis Jones's boy runs ahead, he does not see his father's crumpled body.
He looks up to see the kites fall slowly, crookedly toward blood.

II

Sixty years later we stand in the union hall near a bleached Republic Steel sign.
The hall creaks and moans, a ratty velvet curtain is backdrop for the speakers.
Ed Sadlowski says, *We'll never forget what happened here.*

Old men clap, shift weight, raise trembling hands, sing *Solidarity Forever.*
The workers shuffle to the catered luncheon, eat pizza at dark tables,
then walk into the afternoon where once a pale sky
rained kites, helpless in the plundered air.

The Horses Run Back to Their Stalls

LINDA GREGERSON

It's another sorry tale about class in America, I'm sure
        you're right,
    but you have to imagine how proud we were.

Your grandfather painted a banner that hung from Wascher's
        Pub
    to Dianis's Grocery across the street: Reigh Count,

Kentucky Derby Winner, 1928.
        And washtubs filled
    with French champagne. I was far too young

to be up at the stables myself, of course, it took
        me years
    to understand they must have meant in *bottles*

in the washtubs, with ice.
        His racing colors
    were yellow and black, like the yellow

cabs, which is how Mr. Hertz first made the money
        that built
    the barns that bred the horses, bred at last this perfect

horse, our hundred and thirty seconds of flat-out earth-
        borne bliss.
    They bought the Arlington Racetrack then and Jens

got a job that for once in his life allowed him to pay
        the mortgage
    and the doctors too, but he talked the loose way even

good men talk sometimes and old man Hertz
        was obliged
    to let him go. It was August when the cab strike in

Chicago got so ugly. Somebody must have tipped
                  them off,
          since we learned later on that the Count

and the trainer who slept in his stall had been moved
                  to another
          barn. I'll never forget the morning after: ash

in the air all the way to town and the smell of those
                  poor animals,
          who'd never harmed a soul. There's a nursery

rhyme that goes like that, isn't there? Never
                  did us any
          harm. I think it's about tormenting a cat.

38 Easy Steps to Carlyle's Everlasting Yea

JOHN GUZLOWSKI

After living with Rod McKuen in the horse-filled streets of Sandusky
Arise and sing naked
And dance naked
And visit your mother naked
And be nervous and tragic and plugged in

And pay the waiter in kisses
And pay the beggar in silver
And embrace the silent and scream for them
And grab watches and ask them for directions
And be a carpenter and redeem all the sins of the University of Illinois in Chicago
And look for Walt Whitman beneath the concrete in the street
And put your thumbs in your ears and ask somebody to dance
      The bossa nova and hear him or her say
      Sorry, I left my carrots at home

And eat/write/cry/drink/smoke/laugh and keep holy the Lord's Day all in the same breath
And ride in subways, whistling at every stop for no reason whatsoever
And stroll along Michigan Avenue with your arms around your comrade, the sky

And be a blue angelic tricycle
And be any martyr's unused coffin
And be you or me—it doesn't matter which
And write poems like Pablo Neruda does
And throw them into the street/into the wind

And be Christ waiting at the bus stop for a passing crucifixion
      and not having enough exact change to mount the cross
And be a mail clerk at Sears and send free TV sets to all the charity wards
      at Cook County Hospital
And free the masses and free yourself from the masses
And march on Moscow, searching with burnt-out eyes for Zhivago
And be afoot with your vision
And be afoot with my vision
And be underfoot and underground

And sell magic sparrows at the Maxwell Street Flea Market
And carry flowers to the poets' corner and water them with enormous Byronic tears
And wander through midday downtown Chicago humming the "St. Louis Blues"
And wear your best strawberry hat all night long
And know the meaning of nothing
And guess the meaning of everything
And be a mind-blistered astronaut with nothing to say to the sun but
    Honey, I'm yours.

Bible Belt

TERRY HAMILTON-POORE

Before the move to the stranglehold
of salvation that would not save me—
busing and thin-veiled racism,
pines and blue laws and rusty clay,
cold bedroom, bookish ghost-life
where I shrank and shrank and shrank—

before that I stood with friends broad-shouldered
in Chicago's wind and raced the high-circling light—
the cop to our robbers—
across the hard-pounded playground dirt,
running barefoot on broken glass with our thick,
impervious soles.

There, in that fearful freedom, time and again
we saved ourselves.

The Woman Hanging from the Thirteenth Floor Window

JOY HARJO

She is the woman hanging from the 13th floor
window. Her hands are pressed white against the
concrete moulding of the tenement building. She
hangs from the 13th floor window in east Chicago,
with a swirl of birds over her head. They could
be a halo, or a storm of glass waiting to crush her.

She thinks she will be set free.

The woman hanging from the 13th floor window
on the east side of Chicago is not alone.
She is a woman of children, of the baby, Carlos,
and of Margaret, and of Jimmy who is the oldest.
She is her mother's daughter and her father's son.
She is several pieces between the two husbands
she has had. She is all the women of the apartment
building who stand watching her, watching themselves.

When she was young she ate wild rice on scraped down
plates in warm wood rooms. It was in the farther
north and she was the baby then. They rocked her.

She sees Lake Michigan lapping at the shores of
herself. It is a dizzy hole of water and the rich
live in tall glass houses at the edge of it. In some
places Lake Michigan speaks softly, here, it just sputters
and butts itself against the asphalt. She sees
other buildings just like hers. She sees other
women hanging from many-floored windows
counting their lives in the palms of their hands
and in the palms of their children's hands.

She is the woman hanging from the 13th floor window
on the Indian side of town. Her belly is soft from
her children's births, her worn levis swing down below
her waist, and then her feet, and then her heart.
She is dangling.

The woman hanging from the 13th floor hears voices.
They come to her in the night when the lights have gone
dim. Sometimes they are little cats mewing and scratching
at the door, sometimes they are her grandmother's voice,
and sometimes they are gigantic men of light whispering
to her to get up, to get up, to get up. That's when she wants
to have another child to hold onto in the night, to be able
to fall back into dreams.

And the woman hanging from the 13th floor window
hears other voices. Some of them scream out from below
for her to jump, they would push her over. Others cry softly
from the sidewalks, pull their children up like flowers and gather
them into their arms. They would help her, like themselves.

But she is the woman hanging from the 13th floor window,
and she knows she is hanging by her own fingers, her
own skin, her own thread of indecision.

She thinks of Carlos, of Margaret, of Jimmy.
She thinks of her father, and of her mother.
She thinks of all the women she has been, of all
the men. She thinks of the color of her skin, and
of Chicago streets, and of waterfalls and pines.
She thinks of moonlight nights, and of cool spring storms.
Her mind chatters like neon and northside bars.
She thinks of the 4 A.M. lonelinesses that have folded
her up like death, discordant, without logical and
beautiful conclusion. Her teeth break off at the edges.
She would speak.

The woman hangs from the 13th floor window crying for
the lost beauty of her own life. She sees the
sun falling west over the grey plane of Chicago.
She thinks she remembers listening to her own life
break loose, as she falls from the 13th floor
window on the east side of Chicago, or as she
climbs back up to claim herself again.

Uncle Danny Brags About Playing Special Teams for the '85 Bears

DERRICK HARRIELL

Son, don't be fooled by the frailty of this frame
or graveyard of charred butts lying next to that old bottle
of Thunderbird, I was a fast Negro in '85.
I started that shuffle dance one morning
after jogging into practice with a hangover
and Run DMC record in my head,
I gyrated my legs until a new jive had arrived.
It was me who named him Sweetness
one Mississippi Fall. While he sprinted up the grass,
a fine-ass cheerleader intercepted my eyes,
brother next to me tapped my side,
asked what do you call that,
Sweetness   I whispered.

Dearborn North Apartments

LOLA HASKINS

Chicago, Illinois

Rows of rectangles rise, set into brick.
And in every rectangle, there is a lamp.
Why should there be a lamp in every window?
Because in all this wide city, there is not
enough light. Because the young in the world
are crazy for light and the old are afraid
it will leave them. Because whoever you are,
if you come home late but it looks like noon,
you won't tense at the click as you walk in
which is probably after all only the heat
coming on, or the floorboards settling.
So when you fling your coat to its peg in
the hall, and kick off your heels, and unzip
your black velvet at that odd vee'd angle as if
someone were twisting your arm from behind,
then reach inside the closet for a hanger,
just to the dark left where the dresses live,
what happens next is a complete surprise.

In Michael Robins's class minus one

BOB HICOK

At the desk where the boy sat, he sees the Chicago River.
It raises its hand.
It asks if metaphor should burn.
He says fire is the basis for all forms of the mouth.
He asks, why did you fill the boy with your going?
I didn't know a boy had been added to me, the river says.
Would you have given him back if you knew?
I think so, the river says, I have so many boys in me,
       I'm worn out stroking eyes looking up at the day.
Have you written a poem for us? he asks the river,
       and the river reads its poem,
       and the other students tell the river
       it sounds like a poem the boy would have written,
       that they smell the boy's cigarettes
       in the poem, they feel his teeth
       biting the page.
And the river asks, did this boy dream of horses?
       because I suddenly dream of horses, I suddenly dream.
They're in a circle and the river says, I've never understood
       round things, why would leaving come back
       to itself?
And a girl makes a kiss with her mouth and leans it
       against the river, and the kiss flows away
       but the river wants it back, the river makes sounds
       to go after the kiss.
And they all make sounds for the river to carry to the boy.
And the river promises to never surrender the boy's shape
       to the ocean.

American Apocalypse

EDWARD HIRSCH

Chicago, 1871

It was as if God had taken a pen of fire
      Into his flaming blue hand
   And scrawled a chapter of horrors
         Across the city at night,
Burning the world in a day-and-a-half. . . .

It was as if, after 98 days of drought,
      The furious oranges and reds
   Of the Last Judgment erupted
         In a barn on DeKoven Street:
God had burnished the Gem on the Prairie.

Fire seethed through the shams and shingles,
      Through the parched bodies
   Of cottages and sheds, of cow-stables,
         Corn-cribs, and pigsties,
All the tinder-dry precincts of Garden City.

The raised sidewalks were piles of kindling-
      Sticks under pine and hemlock
   Fences, the shanties were logs
         Lit by kerosene. The barns
Were giant ovens exploding in a lumbermill.

The heavens blazed and a husky southern wind
      Turned into a mass of devils
   Whirling through the streets,
         Advancing in a column
Of smoke and a wall of flame, a steady torrent

Of sparks and a shuddering wave of lightning
      Crackling in the air.
   The fire bells clanged and the
         Steamers stood by helplessly.
Soon the fire swept across the sluggish river

That flared like gasoline and seemed to boil
   In the 3,000 degree heat.
  It burned on three sides of the water
      At once, eating bridges and ships.
The huge grain elevators stacked along the banks.

First, the Tar Works exploded and then came
   The Gas Works and the Armory,
  The police station and the fire house,
      Conley's Patch. There were
Explosions of oil, crashes of falling buildings,

And down came the Post Office and the Water Works,
   The impregnable Board of Trade,
  The Opera House and the Design Academy,
      The sturdy Chamber of Commerce.
Down came the banks, the hotels, the churches. . . .

The tornado of fire rolled toward the north
   And people jammed the streets
  With wagons and carts, with
      Wheelbarrows of belongings.
They came tumbling out of windows and doorways,

Shrieking in all directions. There were horses
   Breathing smoke in dead alleys
  And dogs racing like live torches
      Toward the burning water.
The noise was calamitous, torrential, deafening,

As the world staggered to a last fiery end.
   The firemen might as well
  Have tried to arrest the wind itself
      Since the wind and the fire
Were a single fury hurtling through the night.

The dogs of Hell bounded over the rooftops
   And leaped from tree to tree.
  There were no stars and no clouds,

There was nothing else
In the sky but the fierce vengeance of flames

Flattening the world into stones and ashes.
This was the Great Catastrophe
And some responded to the terror
By kneeling down in embers
And crying out for release from the prophecy:

For behold, the Lord will come in fire and
His chariots like the storm wind
To render his anger in jury
And his rebuke with flames.
For by fire will the Lord execute judgment. . . .

But then the judgment was stayed, the rains
Descended like manna,
Like a fresh pardon from Heaven,
And the winds calmed.
The fire devils died in the arms of the lake

And the wrath abated along the open ground
At the edge of Lincoln Park.
The Great Destruction was over
For the city in ruins.
So this was the smouldering end of Time.

And this was the Lightning City after 36 hours—
A muddy black settlement
On the plains, a ditched fort
After a quick massacre.
This was the Garden of Eden reduced into cinders.

The boom town had become an outpost again.
Soon the army was called in
To save the city from citizens
Who plundered and looted,
And stormed through the rubble in despair.

There were those who set themselves on fire,
    Those who fled together
  On the first trains heading east,
       Those who cursed and wept
For the lost civilization on the prairie.

But there were also the unrepentant ones
    Who were young and free
  Of history at last. They moved
      Through the ruins alone
In a jubilant new world blazing under the sun.

They stood in the cooling ashes without grief
    And imagined their future
  Rising out of the blue lake as
      A man-made mountain range,
A city that aspired upward toward the sky.

Dear John Dillinger,

JOHN WESLEY HORTON

We could rearrange our faces, shave our fingerprints, leave
our legends carved across the walls that we escaped from.
We still wouldn't find ourselves motor-mouthing
across the Silver Screen, translated by Warner or MGM.

I'm impressed—not by how you knocked over
so many banks, spent so many chilly nights in barns
regretting all the hearts you'd broken, the one farm
you'd never return to, the fallow fields, clover
turning blushing cheeks to sunrise, but how you courted
the vanishing act, laid low in the North Woods
just to turn up in Arizona; an alias, a carnival mask,
bullets for teeth and already gone. If everyone believes

you're someone else, you might be born to fly
away from dime store shelves, away from leading men
shooting insults at the cops, who started off as shadows
anyhow. But don't tell me how they shadowed you.

Don't tell me about a lady in red, about G-Men
breaking all the rules, the rock-hot concrete of Chicago
sidewalks, the flashbulb's powder pop. I'd rather

you hadn't lost. I'd rather buy the myth—how you burned
those mortgages in the banks, paid off
so many failing farms. Things might be easier then.
I could pack my bags, believing
around the corner was a place. I could make another life.

on the other end. right there

RANDALL HORTON

i am up through everyplace music reaches.
a little further out from there i watch breaking
waves crash manmade sand along lakeshore.
the water beckons me to come swim & i become
awakened by coldness each stroke i am tuned
downward then i lift upward to a rising crescendo.
deep, the undercurrent clamps my ankles, dragging
river bottom, perhaps a rail of bone, in another longitude
i could have come from darkness holds the light
skimming over rugged surfaces, i bob but
surface again, my eyes strain to see sound
echo a piano rippling flügelhorn: blow: i breathe.
out over the next wave break back at chicago
i look, this forward motion is a soundtrack.

My Great-Grandfather Takes a Business Trip, c. 1912

ANN HUDSON

Let's say it happened in spring. Let's say
it was a cold spring, the snow late on the ground
and the trees budding regardless.
We know he took the train north to Chicago
for business; let's say pressed, cuffed trousers,
white shirt, a narrow four-in-hand. An overcoat
lined for early spring. Let's say he kissed his wife,
who he called Queenie, and nodded at his two
young children. Then he latched the door
behind him and strode away. Years later
one of his five sisters thought she saw him
across a crowded restaurant. She called his name
and the man turned and stared, then crumpled
his paper napkin and hurried out. Is it better to believe
he abandoned his family so successfully the police
and a private investigator never found
a trace of him, his wallet, his clothes, even
the train ticket we assume he used, just a ring
of keys on Halsted? Or better to believe
he was mugged, and hauled away
before he could be discovered? Or that he threw himself
into the south branch of the Chicago River,
his breathing quick and shallow, his ears, lips,
and fingers blueing, unable soon to hear the automobiles
rattling over the Halsted bridge above him
as he slid, like any garbage, away?

Road Trip

DONALD ILLICH

Three college dudes, six hours,
a trip from Ohio, drunk,
Chicago has the best pizza,
as soon as they arrive there,
jumping into the lake, January
waves knocking them back,
soaking their jeans, t-shirts,
pants pebbled with sand,
That was freakin' freezing!
one has business in town,
pawnshop guitar, phone calls,
Northwestern search for friends,
failing, guitar lost, impossible,
eyes encrusted, half asleep,
at Giordano's, in a booth,
digesting a slice, deep dish,
thick as the weariness in
their eyes, *This was worth it!*
Damn good! Back to highways,
a stop for gas, danger, bad
side of town, nothing happens,
the strangers all ignore them,
the dudes arrive at their dorm,
still hungry, *When are donuts*
ready at the store? the lake
a memory, rushing somewhere
they hadn't been before,
to feel cold, human, shaking,
no longer alone in the flow
of water that people pass by,
ignoring its power to kill
or to bring together in love.

Luminaria

LARRY JANOWSKI

Chicago eats light, sucks it in
like a black hole, hoards it
like a radium dial planning
to stay awake all night because
light—like the grass and flesh
we devour—decays. We
need more. Always. But
unlike broad green leaves
that take their sun straight,
we cannot look full on light
and live. We need the tempering
of angels, moons, or cities
lest we go blind and starve.

Yet there's light enough today
to squander: towers toy with it,
canyon walls, fluid as melting
sand, play lunch hour catch,
pitch a gleam underhand to brush
against your hair, like a secret stare
in a jammed subway car
that leaves you blushing
and blessed. This city's glass
slabs light your path
in the dark valley. They square off,
gather broken suns
in their thousand panes
to flatter in shadowless
light your unsuspecting face—
you never expect
that single beam to snag
the corner of your eye,
like the glint of a white bird
alight upon your sleeve.

Dear Chicago—

PHILIP JENKS AND SIMONE MUENCH

On election night, this grid of yours
was love blown to lava. Lit up by onions
& fireworks, a delirium of this plus that.
Did you read Max Weber's postcard about you?
Your smoky sediment; your shouldered sonata.
You are smaller in person but shimmer
on camera. Burning at a distance we walk
into you: falling glass, lake effects & electricity—
a Midwest lesson on skyscraper elation.
Perfect spot for *Henry: Portrait of a Serial Killer*
& adoptive home to Nelson, Gwendolyn & Studs.
What else do you name children living near aqueducts?

How on earth are you doing, Chicago?
Your eloquent 90/94 gouged us in two.
Will you piece that together for us, Chicago?
We still love the elongation of your body
against the frosted lake; ice is the new modernism.
Once meat. Now, you shudder
your crocuses in ground faux new-age storefronts,
stuffed abundant flatness under this lithography
of bodies. This intimate ethnography:
a human being with its skin removed.
Both city "on the make" & "on the take."
You are contradictory & quarrelsome
—*as full of crooks as a saw with teeth*—
yet you are also a glorious canary-filled clarity
breathing change in a young, but stumped, century.

One likes to think Chicago

THOMAS L. JOHNSON

might have gone at least a little
wild that night during the Depression
when the slimmed-down young singer
fresh from New York finished
her first set as headliner with Fletcher
Henderson's band at the Grand Terrace Club.

But they didn't. Hadn't a clue
who she was or what she could do
as an artist. Hadn't been told.
Nor had they an inkling she and her mom
had left all they possessed back East,
counting on making it big, recreating
themselves in this new windy mecca.

That evening, her opening night,
the Grand Terrace patrons failed to respond.
They listened, or not, and took her or left her
without any fuss. Without anything.

After the show, the manager, furious
she'd failed to connect with his clubgoers,
told her she stank up the place, wasn't worth
what he'd promised to pay her per week
(seventy-five), and finally shouted her
out of his office. Before leaving,
she picked up an inkwell, threw it at him,
and threatened to kill him.

Later, the only number from this gig
Billie Holiday cared to remember
was the first one she sang, when she
sensed right away no one there
understood her singing: Malneck and Mercer's
bittersweet "If You Were Mine"
("Yes, even my heart, Even my life,
I'd trade it all for you, And think I was lucky too
If you were mine").

The Jewel

RICHARD JONES

I like this moment when there is nothing
more I need to do,
when I have emptied
everything on the counter—
eggs, bread, apples, and some chocolate
I will give my children after homework—
and I am free to study
the checkout lady's red face
ever so slightly gasping for air,
the quick hands of the teen-aged boy
distractedly bagging groceries,
and the lady behind me so tiny
she stands on tiptoes to empty her cart.
I have all the time in the world
to open my wallet and count bills
for the Salvation Army bell ringer
standing outside the automatic glass doors
in the dark and falling snow,
time even to survey the sad
faces on the magazines
and read the headlines and confessions
and forgive each star by name.
But when everything has been counted
and bagged, the bill calculated
and the receipt handed to me,
I've forgotten where I am and what I'm doing,
so determined am I to see the angels
William Blake tells me
stand among us,
cherubim lingering by the illuminated
bins of produce,
seraphim protecting the fish sticks
in the frozen food section.
The cashier is saying "Sir? Sir?"
but now I am seeking to pierce the veil
that separates us from the saints in heaven.

Gazing out over the rows of shoppers
waiting in lines with their carts,
and now holding up everyone in line behind me,
I am squinting to find my father, who loved fish sticks,
to see him in his appointed place
among the multitudes of angels and saints,
the heavenly choirs
I can almost hear
singing to me.

Chicago Noise (Love Letter to Steve Albini)

JARRET KEENE

How many boys want to be whipped by Steve Albini's guitar?
—Sonic Youth bassist/singer Kim Gordon

Woke up this morning, as usual, hungry for white-boy noise and black
coffee. Popped in—what else?—Big Black's Songs About *!?king
and blasted it at full volume on the home stereo so I could feel every

drum-machined wallop in my molars, every lacerating riff against
my face, those places where noise really hits me when its good
and loud. Steve, there's something about your band Big Black

in the morning that helps me to more effectively hate birds outside
my window as they chirp ridiculous tunes about nothing to no one,
something in the serrated edges of the song "Pavement Saw" and

the slaughterhouse fury of "Colombian Necktie" that transports me
to the Loop, jostling around inside a metal tube across an ice-cold,
urban-Midwest landscape of old, bombed-out meatpacking plants.

Like it's a clear day in March and I'm taking it all in—the canyons
of LaSalle, the cliffs of Michigan Avenue, the public artworks—
and there's this satanic chainsaw behind my ears, eager to sink

its teeth into my skull, turning my lights out and then everyone
else's. This noise is dirty and yet so pure that I can't help feeling
even more comfortable in my alienation, even happier in hostile

territory. I imagine myself lying down like a lamb at the paws
of a lion guarding the stairs of the Art Institute. I picture myself
walking into a Wicker Park record shop (a real record shop that

actually sells, you know, vinyl) and asking the skinny, unfriendly
employees there if they might sell me another Big Black LP. And
when they scowl at me with an expression that says "Why don't

you already own that record, poser?" all I can say to my fellow rock
snobs is leave me alone, because I'm armed and dangerous,
and about to vaporize Cloud Gate in Millennium Park, to rip

the girders from Calder's red-orange flamingo-looking thing perched
in front of the Federal Center with my incisors before flame-broiling it
oh-so-slowly with an acetylene torch until the steel is tender enough

to eat with a plastic spork, to challenge the next thrash band
to play the Double Door to a demolition derby-style mosh pit
involving broken beer bottles and our bare chests and bags of salt.

And if anyone asks about the point of this tsunami of sucking nihilism,
this whole tortured carnival ride, let me say that it's my chance to
ignore the terrifying silence at the end of this caffeinated daydream.

Anyhow, Steve, just thought I'd write you a quick letter letting you
know how much your anti-corporate band gets me dreaming
of Chicago and prepares me for another gray and greasy day

of corporate enslavement, chained to my cubicle, hoping for a
moment to shut down my computer and loosen my tie, straining
to hear a measure, the merest note, of the sweet music of birds.

Miniature Church

SUSAN KELLY-DEWITT

The Thorne Miniatures, Chicago, 1998

To enter, crouch
on your own eyebeam.
To genuflect, shrink.

Even this small
your Father in Heaven
expects it.

He's hidden now
like a secret camera
in his risen dead

Son's pint-sized
heart, in the grain
of the minuscule

crucifix, the star
thistle-sized thorns.
Marvelous!

how the minute
stigmata camouflages
the immense

suffering,
like moth's eyespots.
(Even the misguided

fly squeezed
in between stained
glass slats

must think
with the mind
of a midge or gnat.)

One faux crumb
of shellacked
grace waits

to come alive
on a Hummel
tongue. How gothic

a replica worship is.
When the universe
boomerangs back

from the existential,
this wee church
will be ready.

There's even a baby
spoon of plastic holy
water in the vestibule

to pretend a blessing.

Under the Terrible Burden of Destiny Laughing as a Young Man Laughs

BECCA KLAVER

November 4, 2008

Will the mannequins come to life
Will the sky crack and drip yolk
Will the machinery catch on itself
Will the bloody pocket kerchief read *mandate*
Will the circle be unbroken
Will the manatees burst through the glass
Will the cement shake and shriek
Will Sue clamber anciently toward the green
Will the darkness drop again
Will somebody please help us
Will the shadows of desert birds reel
Will the skyline stand
Will Studs be a benevolent god
Will the experiment work

The Rainiest Day in Recorded Chicago History

SUSANNA LANG

It was a taste of Armageddon, almost a simulation—not Galveston, no one is
    writing a ballad about us.
But where the expressway dips under a viaduct, cars rose to the surface of the
    water like whalefish,
and on the northwest side of the city, streets were barricaded, police cars
    parked crosswise with lights flashing,
a helicopter hovered overhead, everyone out on the bridge—families with
    their babies in strollers, flocks of sparrows.
Thirty-eight people moved to a shelter, carrying their belongings in white
    plastic bags, carrying their grandmothers, their children, three dogs and
    a cat.
A few gravestones floated down Milwaukee Avenue, escapees from St.
    Adalbert Cemetery.
There were pictures in the paper, men with their hair slicked down, shoulders
    bent under the weight of sandbags
which did not keep the river from breaking and entering the houses along
    North Monticello and North Avers.
The Water Reclamation District opened the sluice gates and the river
    catapulted into the lake,
home again after more than a century, longer than the Cubs have been
    dreaming of another World Series.
Everywhere in town, the river's edges were blurred: the land half water, the
    water gripping the roots of trees,
and outside of town, the Des Plaines River, the Fox, the Salt Creek, St. Joseph
    Creek, all rose up in celebration,
in triumph over the restraints we had placed on them, somersaulting and
    gliding through the haunts of their youth.
Despite our fears (carseats in our arms as we stood by the highway), despite
    the stink, despite our ruined carpets,
it was hard not to join in the party, not to acknowledge the rightness of rivers
    running like rivers
and boys leaping the picnic tables in Caldwell Woods, riding the surface of the
    water like a gaggle of Huck Finns on a raft.

At the Palmer House Hilton

ELIZABETH LANGEMAK

In the drawer: a Bible,
in the bed, the scent of a bed

that can barely bear to be
unmade. To sleep we nearly slice

it open, our legs skimming across
pure sheets. Of course we cannot

stay here, of course this desk
could not stand work; no service

could sustain us long. Sunday
brings the summons slipped

beneath the door and we will haul
our bags in answer but until

then, we have this hollow
Eden with its view of slighter roofs

and each afternoon, white towels
blooming like fruit on the rack.

dead dead

QURAYSH ALI LANSANA

heat on the southside

I.

last night, police cordoned the four square
blocks surrounding my house in pursuit of a thug
who unloaded on the shell of a gangsta
in the funeral parlor filled with formaldehyde
and lead. black folks scattered, staining
complicated streets. i settle in for summer:
the maze to the front door, running teens
smelling of weed and tragedy from my stoop
reminding my sons they are not sources
of admiration, praying that might change. not yet
june heat rises like the murder rate, gleam
and pop already midnight's bitter tune.

II.

fifteen years ago, tyehimba jess
told me about a funeral home
with a drive-through window.

you pull up, push a call button
through bulletproof glass a friendly
somber attendant takes your request.

moments later, casket open
your order appears for review.

at the time i thought it inhumane.
now i think about the abstraction
of friendship while counting bullets.

III.

is there an extra dead?
what is the term for dying again
when already? killing chi?

and what of the corpses that walk
my block in the anonymity
of black skin and white tees
filled with fluid.

At the Sea Lion Pool

ANNA LEAHY

Lincoln Park Zoo, Chicago, Illinois

My younger sister and I
open our little pink mouths
and place our tiny lips
to our helium-filled balloons
in the French kisses
we won't know for years:
aarrrph, aarrrph, we bark
from our lowest register
as if we can talk
to the gray and harbor seals
in their own blubbery voices,
as if we are bigger than our bodies
and can be taken seriously,
as if we, like the seals, want
someone to compete for us
so that we can each hold
a fertilized egg deep inside
until another summer, timing
our offspring like seals do
for a summer like this one
we share at the zoo
by the vast expanse of lake
under our skyscrapered landscape.

Chicago: City of Neighborhoods

VIOLA LEE

Ask me to define
this city in which I live.

Ask me to define
this city of neighborhoods,

this city of backgrounds,
of wind and rain,

of cold winter months,
of light, and of ages ago.

Ask me to define
my parents, two friends

who fell in love here.
I love thinking

of the two of them,
together,

taking the El
to the various ends

of the city: admiring
the glass on the south side,

the water
on the north side,

the air on the west side
and then come four.

No better skyline,
my father will often

hesitate and say
in his broken English.

Well, I speak
broken English as well:

this is the language
of the city in which I live,

the language
where I first learned

these words, the language
where I learned

about movement, desire,
sound. Ask me

to define Korean food
and Western Avenue

and the Korean
grocery store

on Kimball. In back,
a run-down diner

where old Korean women
are making my food

while I walk around
with a rusty cart filled

with dried seaweed,
tofu and a bag of white rice.

Ask me to define
this city in which I live.

Ask me to define the word,
place. Ask me

to define that quiet room
in the Art Institute

framed by clay pots
and columns. Ask me

to define space:
the Bloomingdale Trail,

Cloud Gate,
the Chicago Picasso,

Cultural Center,
skyscraper,

Damen Avenue,
Devon Avenue,

Lawrence Avenue,
the Blue Line,

the Red Line, Loyola.
Ask me to define

the word,
boulevard: Humboldt,

Washington, Logan.
Ask me to define

this city in a last name:
Lee, Oh, Klaus,

Lillig, Kalina,
Huh, Greenwood,

Shin, Park,
Daley, Roe, Ategou,

Morrison, Nyderek,
O'Brien, Rashid,

Harkins, Brookes,
Berson, Amankwa,

rebirth, light.
Ask me to define

this city, my name,
my family, my home,

my nieces and nephews
in just a few words:

Korea, Ireland, Israel,
Philippines, Germany,

Togo, Costa Rica. Ask me
to define their light,

their eyes,
my temperature

will rise,
one day, one day.

Ask me to define
the city in which I live,

this city of neighborhoods,
the city where we speaking

      broken English.

Emerald Ash

BRENNA LEMIEUX

In the thickening citydusk, early ash blossoms cling to
branches like my grandmother's cursive—the pattern
and hues of a dress I'd wear to elope. Near home, strangers
clutter my sidewalk, chatter in languages as indecipherable
as rain prattling to puddles. For a moment, I wonder whether
my mind is leaking away like my grandmother's did, so that
we whispered *dementia* and quietly pocketed her car keys.

> That spring, my sister and I drove the Oldsmobile to school,
> rode home along Charles Street. She found a bottle of dish soap
> jammed beneath the seats, squeezed a green palmful, reached
> out the window and spread her slimy fingers—a trail of bubbles,
> as if we'd commandeered a submarine.

> At six, I caught Fifth disease and sprouted a fever, grew
> a red rash that spilled its ink across my arms and chest,
> itched like lace worn too close to the skin. My father poured
> water over me in the bathtub. It warbled, pooled against
> the porcelain. When I sang along, he called the doctor.

> But even soap cannot cure some diseases—not when it's poured
> into a washer set to delicate, not when it's dripping from
> splayed fingers out the window of a car, not when it's rubbed
> to suds and spread across the skin with a cotton cloth.

Inside now, the ceiling leak means the upstairs neighbors
are bathing. I flick on the radio; static scrapes against
static before I find a voice: the reporter warns that
Emerald Ash Borers have crept into Chicago to chew
and hollow our trees, so we can't tell they're dying until
their bark rots, until they crumple under the weight of rain.

Seasonality of Violence

FRANCESCO LEVATO

The following is a thumbnail sketch.

Relationships   important in the aggregate

    require a complex answer,

    these patterns of change over time.

Does one racial/ethnic, gender, or age group prey
on another.

    If we assume, for the sake of argument,
take data at face value

    seasonal fluctuation is tendency

.22 caliber rifle, kitchen knife, baseball bat

    some are more likely inside residence, than not.

Location refers to place   where body was found

    "floaters" in Lake Michigan,
the trunks of cars at O'Hare

the unit of analysis is the victim, this presence
treated as question.

Note: The text of the poem is taken from *Specification of Patterns Over Time in Chicago Homicide: Increases and Decreases, 1965–1981.*

Chicago Noir

GARY COPELAND LILLEY

blues tribute to Motherwell

Western Ave: leaving the blue line
I can't name the tune
the National Steel guitar and street traffic
are playing but I remember dancing to it.
Her hip, right side, the near back,
above the waistline a tattoo
of black ink; the shoot of irises
I've held in my hands.

A man doesn't know anything
until he's breathed air at least 30 years —
what he knows then
is that he knows nothing. I am not
the priest of the modern drama
but I can tell you every mistake
I think I've made. My qualified heart
has been going off like a car alarm.

Doctor Feelgood says I may get better,
baby, just not sure I'll ever be well.
I thought this alluring woman was gone.
Gave her logical reasons to leave
a middle-age man. The concern,
she's almost too-much younger,
a million shades of blues have been sung
about being in such a situation.

In the dim golden light of Rosa's club,
during the whiskey solo and complements
of smoke and harmonica,
I lean towards her. She's been waiting
for this and comes to meet me.
The amazing glory of now, our mouths,
just one of her ways in proving
that the main rule of love is to not be dead.

Too Much to Take In

MOIRA LINEHAN

The long pulpy fibers of scrolls absorb dyes unevenly.
—Exhibition notes.

Now it's Chicago I explore
without you. Home for a month—this

cavernous room, view of brick backs
of old buildings, newer high-rises

in the distance, reflecting glass.
Will I ever write a poem

where grief doesn't surface? Twelve stories
below, at intersections, shaded

canyons stretch between skyscrapers.
To show this woman hunched over

a blank page, I'd use very little
ink, just the tip of a dry brush.

How Should Chicago Be Governed?[1]

RACHEL LODEN

I walk through the valley of Chi where death is
Top floor, the view alone will leave you breathless Uhhhh!
—Kanye West

Oh Chicago   never stop being weird with your Casimir Pulaski
oh Chicago! Current mood: excited

Glitter is a killa in Chi tizzle
You are such a flirt with your Loose Leaf Lounge

Chicago you make me silly with your lake effect
If I walk my dog in Wrigleyville

And a green river in March is strangely pleasing
All mysteries are explained by the phrase "Oh, we must be in Cicero!"

Okay Chicago   you're not making me happy
I guard my parking space with an old chair and an unusable broom

O most beautiful and most ungovernable of cities
And then it was like, *oh, Chicago.* So I think it's just Chicago's turn

---

[1]Title of a book by my great-grandfather, Bartow A. Ulrich (Hazlitt & Co., 1893).

Fermata Chicago

MARTY McCONNELL

when the bricklayer lifts his daughter to bed
and the Irish lullaby trickles down the stairs
of their Albany Park house and the Columbian

gardener three doors down stirs in her lotus
pose and at the El station the crackheads
lean shirtless against the bricks still warm

from the day, the city nestles into its potholes,
the sun remembers her crush on the lake
and goes down past the ferris wheel, past the joggers

in their mismatched track suits and road-worn
shoes, past the billboards and the cars just now
flicking on their headlights, a parade of habit

and long want, of what's for dinner and how
many days left like this one, before summer comes
with her rowdy tastes and riotous nights—how many

dusks left when the best dream you can make
is also what waits at the far end of Lake Shore Drive,
a cold beer and a warm steak, or hot collard greens

and the raccoons haven't come back to the attic,
the kids have already had their baths and smell
of soap and finished homework, or the girls

are waiting at the L&L with two-dollar lagers
and last weekend's stories sweating to be told
as the waitress grinds the toe of her new pump

against the stub of her first break cigarette
and the sidewalk, a column of beige coats
filing past will call at the Victory Gardens, the train

rolling past here in the middle of everywhere, night
coming on, some god holding his breath as if passing
a cemetery, as if to win a bet, as if answering a dare.

Sandburg Variations

CAMPBELL McGRATH

I. Early Spring

Money courses through Chicago's veins like the essence urging the redbuds into bloom, tulips made wiser by the memory of snow, template of April and the daffodils paper-hung, bereft, the white whale of winter rendered unto fat. And May, the grape hyacinth, apple blossom—and the rain ruining the west-facing azaleas while the north facing azaleas have yet to bloom. You can feel it pulsing along the industrious avenues, viscid, luxuriant, explosively amoral—the old neighborhood flush with it now, the industrial bakery—"Golden Hearth"— torn down, sad tracts of mud and cinders behind barbed-wire, as if cairns of crumbled brick required care and protection. Like an animal breathing, veins of a leaf running with sap, engine of effulgence, resurgent, branches and limbs and roots and blossoms, a force beyond reason, or ruthlessly reasonable.

II. Prairie School

Chicago's magnificent cubic scatter across the snow-sketched prairie,
its arrowing ascension and continental horizontality,
its railyard conjury and truckway bricollage,
its voluble thrum of human self-assurance—
discourse of happenstance or absolute mastery,
monologue of the jackal as known on Kedzie, Pulaski, Cicero,
street rant of the prophet roaming those wide, western avenues
cloaked in an aurora of enlightenment or psychosis.

III. Aubade

Which among us has never heard the music of traffic taking wing, shades and variations of a logarithmic chord, song of the city like a message from within? Who could fail the summons of yon quite visible smokestacks aglint through gray inutterable vapors this peculiarly unparticular morn? Where is he who does not bear the scars of shingle nails upon a tattered thumb, the tar of Stinky Weinberg's stooped roof, laundromats raped and looted by streetlights, buses smoked to fitful ashes, night's metropolis melted down and recast? Song of the city like a terrible job, nail-gunning sheetrock in a West Loop heat wave, late shift with a push broom in a clockless terminal, hustling cocktails at zero hour

when the sour beads of fear drop like pearl onions into every glass of beer and
watered whiskey along the rail, sad drunks eating pickled eggs, loneliness worn
like the robes of a prize fighter, rags and bones, rags and what?

IV. For Those Begging Spare Change outside the Chicago Board of Trade

The ghosts of Chicago are not immaterial, they are not sad or lost.
They wander among us, worldly and explicit.
They fear the hawk and speak respectfully of the mayor.

Hoping for nickels their laces flap open, pockets full
of pint bottles and luckless Lotto tickets.

Numbers do not tell their story, nor the rattle
of disconsolate coins in paper cups,
nor sleek commuter trains departing modern stations,
nor the wall behind them with its monument to men at work
in a more just republic and a century of simpler labor.

Their song is not the wind but an insistent click of longing
I've heard all day, every block of the city, every footfall,
until, on a bench near the lake at evening,
I discover embedded in the heel of my boot
a battered lapel pin in the shape of an American flag.

How to Hear Chicago

PAUL MARTÍNEZ POMPA

Here a spirit must yell
to be heard yet a bullet

need only whisper to make
its point—sometimes I imagine

you right before your death
with an entire city in your ears.

Jack Johnson Comes to Chicago

ADRIAN MATEJKA

I was out of doors, eating snowballs
for dinner & sleeping by Lake Michigan
in January. Nights so cold even

the Chicago police weren't up for rousting
me. The soles of my shoes were so
thin, I could step on a dime & tell

whether it was heads or tails. Frank
Childs bringing me on for sparring
was my first bit of Chicago luck. They

used to call Frank "The Crafty Texan,"
but I still haven't met a colored Texan
who wasn't crafty. What wasn't lucky:

the sparring itself. In the ring, Frank
pursued me like I'd been friendly
with his wife. He'd grab my shoulder

with his left hand, then hook my ribs
with his right the until his corner man
pulled him off. I was smaller then

& couldn't defense like I can now.
Frank was a big man—all grapple, fast
gloves, & red eyes, but when somebody

told him I needed a place to stay, he
let me sleep on his floor. Then his no
good wife came back. It was the middle

of the night, snowing so hard the brick
buildings wanted shelter. Even if I'd
been flush, most of the Chicago hotels

didn't board coloreds. Thanks to Frank's
sweetie, I spent that night underneath
a statue of General John A. Logan.

It was so cold, it seemed as if
the bronze horse the General sat on
turned his head away from the wind.

Chicago

ERIKA MIKKALO

This summer I am on top of the bus.
The bus is double-decker, big and red.
I dispense tales of drownings, fires, customs
Chicago-specific: pat the lion's head
in front of the Institute—no: stroke tail.
Hands, thousands, have worn patina away.
The traffic at five moves as slow as snails.
Monuments, inevitably, decay.
Slow-chapped lips and time's toothsome jaws
will lick down limestone, mortar, brick and steel
as surely as the marketplace will cause
a creature trapped, fixed on its next meal,
backly forth in an iron cage to pace,
ending just as dead if it wins the race.

Noon outside the Music Mart: A Sestina

WILDA MORRIS

The chorus marches; in gray suit and tie
they come to the courtyard. They pause, then slide
into their folding chairs, in the bright light
of summer sun. The tall conductor, hand-
some and alert, prepares his music.
Secretaries and clerks sit side by side

in the courtyard, happy to be outside.
Once more the conductor fingers his tie,
then signals the choristers. The music
begins, as mellow as a sax or slide
trombone. An unkempt woman stands, one hand
setting down her big bag of chips, as light

and airy as she would like to be light
on her bunioned feet. With the bag beside
her, she tiptoes and turns, raises one hand
and begins dancing. A man whispers, *Tie
her up!* She pirouettes and slides, the slide
of her feet matches the rhythmic music.

Dance steps she learned as a child? What music
permeated her days when life was light
and wondrous, the time before the long slide
into homelessness, when she lived inside
a house, was not bound by a strangling tie;
before her husband turned mean, raised a hand

against her, a booted foot, made her hand
over her dignity—and her music,
saying, *You are worthless, your only tie
is to me. You will always be a light-
weight. You'd better stick by my side,
you bitch, or I will beat you down the slide*

to oblivion. She had strength to slide
out of his life. No one gave her a hand.
It meant living in heat and cold outside
alone with only internal music
of memories. Her possessions were light,
one bag, since then stolen, a broken tie.

We all dance and slide to the music
of life, a hand reaching toward the light.
Stand at her side. Feel a tangible tie.

Ferris wheel at Navy Pier

JULIE PARSON NESBITT

Modeled after the very first Ferris wheel, which was built for Chicago's 1893 World's
Columbian Exposition, the Navy Pier Ferris wheel has 40 gondolas, each seating
up to 6 passengers.

The old pier leans its narrow shoulder against the shifting lake.
From the pier's center the Ferris wheel rises like a strange flower
fifteen stories high, whose petals spin in the slow drift of lake wind.

The Ferris wheel curves toward the leafy north, bows to the smoky south.
Below, a tide of lovers, strollers and children shifts and flows.
Waves slap the pier like a dealer shuffling cards.

The wheel revolves to the sunlit east and spins to the steel west
where black slabs of buildings stab the air. In the wheel's shadows
a girl presses herself along the salt sweat of a boy's thigh.

The Ferris wheel raises clapping hands to the sky.
For seven long minutes the riders rise, crest and descend.
The sun tosses its silver coins to the lake.

Beautiful city, terrible dream.

Lee Smith

JOEY NICOLETTI

. . . the best at smuggling a game into the clubhouse in history.
—Jim Murray

Bearded and brawny,
he grips the ball in his muscular mitt.
And then the throw:
his brown fingers releasing
the ball—pure gas from the shadows
of Wrigley; Darryl Strawberry

swings and hits nothing but air.
Nothing else to do but mutter to himself,
shake his head in the marinated day
as the crowd taunts him back to the dugout,
Darryl, Darryl.
Game over.

A high five from Jody Davis here,
another one from Ryno there;
the stands rattle. The wind pulls a muscle
as fans yell the vine off the outfield wall,
mustard-stained shirts, hot dog smiles, and all.

Journey

BARBRA NIGHTINGALE

It was somewhere on Drexel
near the university—
a big old house, formal
front parlor, long windows of dusk.

Christmas eve, a party—
smoke thick and sweet,
turntable spinning
Country Joe and the Fish.

We were reading *Howl*
and crying, reading
Howl and shouting
above the noise, above the smoke.

On the window seat, a cat
orange as the moon,
the stars of our future
written in his eyes.

If only they'd open,
shut tight as they were—
tight against the light,
the smoke, the endless talk

the years already spent,
regret a word we didn't know.
But I can see it now,
see the points the pupil makes,

the oval liquid shimmer
the convexity of sun,
see the child on the corner
waiting to come in.

I can see the streets—
Eugenie and Wells, Armitage,
Clark—see the scrapes on the walls,
the rust in the dreams.

Of course we were wise
to everything: to flowers
and bread, coffee and purple
stars and moon, any mantra

with *ohm*. Say it *ah-ohhmmm* . . .
legs crossed, palms up
and always the smoke
pungent and sweet.

Yes, I can see the rain
the yellow snow, the tires
and chains, drifts too high,
the angels left behind

like footprints going nowhere,
circles around a tree,
like words left hanging,
left shattered on the ground.

It was me, not you, picked up the pieces
with a ginger-mittened hand,
shoved them slowly, slowly
melting into my pocket.

That pea-blue coat still damp,
dripping in my closet,
the cat long gone.
Just me in the window seat,

Watching the snow.
Where did I go?

Chancing Upon the Manatees

ELISE PASCHEN

The journey's tough:
troughs or else shoals
challenge each crossing.
We navigate
the Avenue:
do we change course
or simply sail
the puddle's ocean?
—"Columbus"

            Steering children across
the Millennium lawn, we hear drums'
rumble, the sirens' caterwauling
across Columbus, and we spy
remains of the parade: a float
decked with teenage girls, dressed in gowns.
Our three explorers, step in time,
rat-a-tat march, their first Columbus
Day parade.
            The year 1493
when Christopher Columbus sighted
three mermaids rising out of ocean,
beyond the coast of Hispaniola.
He noted the discovery
of manatees, West Indian,
from the species *Sirenius,*
lumbering mammals sailors mistook
for sirens waving.

            We pilot our crew
away from the parade, seek higher
terrain and climb the bank to Plensa's
fountain. Our daughter, son, and niece
become transfixed, then splash and wade,
squealing as they discover water.

We pull them from the shallows dripping
from the calves down. Our son kicks off
a shoe.
                    Searching for manatees
in Captiva, our daughter lost
her sneaker, running to the harbor's edge
to spot a meandering creature.
Land-bound, we don't confuse the shy
ponderous sea-cow for a siren.
A shadow navigates between
motorboats, a mistaken mermaid,
on the brink of vanishing from sight.

A World of Our Own

JOHANNY VÁZQUEZ PAZ

to the people of Humboldt Park

Between two flags we built
the past of an island exiled to memory.

We put up colonial balconies
and replaced the asphalt with paving stones,
the parks with plazas,
the supermarkets with *colmados*,
American coffee with *Café Yaucano*,
and hamburgers with steak *jibaritos*.

We changed street names and words in Spanish:
from "desfile" to *parada*, from "patio" to *yarda*,
from "alfombra" to *carpeta*, from "mercado" to *marqueta*,
because we are bilingual *y podemos mezclarlas*.

We put flavor in the food, rhythm
in the music, murals on the walls,
accents on the words, heat into the cold.

We opened *botánicas*, cultural centers,
galleries, museums, restaurants
and anything else we needed
so our children could learn their heritage
of waves returned to shore
mixed with the blood of three races.

We built a world of our own between two flags,
a neighborhood with well known faces, familiar aromas
and noises kept company by the rumble of the drum.

Our homeland in exile that floats like a desert island
in the deep and vast sea of the city of Chicago.

Tracks on the Ground, Tracks in the Sky

TODD JAMES PIERCE

*Tired of producing films, Walt Disney returned to Chicago, where he'd lived as
a teenager, to attend the 1948 Railroad Fair. He was accompanied by his friend
and animator, Ward Kimball.*

For the rest of his life Walt would talk
about the fair, three days captaining steam
along the tracks. The highlight
was pushing an engine
past a hundred
a rumble that shook
the world to a smear.
But in moments of reflection
he knew Chicago was more
than trains. It was smoke twisting
from stacks along the shore.
It was paper clouds sliding across
a cornflower sky. It was streets
leading back to the house
where he'd lived as a boy.

On the final day he asked his friend
to follow him from the fair
to the L
from tracks on the ground
to tracks in the sky.
He wanted a witness
so that months later he could talk
about old Chicago as though his friend
had known it as well. They walked
past his house and the school
where he'd learned to divide. Block
after block, the image of his eyes
matching the image in his heart.
He stopped only once
when he saw that the old bakery
had become a courtyard mall.

How strange, that sight
five shops under a common roof.
As his eyes peered through dark glass
he realized these shops
weren't new, but old:
the countertops worn, the wallpaper
yellow, one hand missing
from the clock on the wall.
He felt it then—
the heaviness of age
the knife of despair
puncturing his heart.
He lowered his eyebrows
in anger
then sensed a warm, heavy hand
on his shoulder, his friend
urging him to continue down
this path of his youth.
Together they stepped from the curb
into blackness
their eyes fixed
on a constellation of moths
imaginary starlight
that circled a single lamp
at the far end of the street.

Plattdeutsch

JAMES PLATH

Beneath the shingles, the copper street haze
of Chicago, the neighborhood women are
speaking in tongues. Ten miles away, farmers
walk to their barns with coffee breath, coughs
like foghorns. Only the milkman and ragman
are out this early to work the Lincoln Square
district, clicking their own tongues to urge
horses along. In one of the brownstones

on Brigham Street, pots and pans clang
in broken English, clunk in dialect. Soon
early morning sidewalks will begin to creak
as old women in babushkas toddle toward
bargains, dragging metal shopping carts behind
them like dinosaur tails. Ahead, the butcher
scatters fresh sawdust on the rough plank
floor, as if he were feeding chickens.

At the two-flat on Brigham, three women stand
by the kitchen table, poised under a bare-bulb
light with knives—a seasonal rite. Behind them,
on the cast-iron stove, with its smell of
beechwood burning orange, a double-boiler
sends steam toward the ceiling that blends with
the scent of blood and onions and curls down
again, like a cow's tongue sampling morning.

"Cut, cut," Oma says, waving her butcher's
knife at the girl who had stopped to wipe her
eyes with the sleeve of her house dress, to stare
at her reflection in the silvery blade. The girl,
my grandmother, watches Oma as she slices away
at the edges of sleep. She wants to do well.
She *must* do well. "Cut, cut," Oma says.
On the table before them is twenty pounds

of fresh-cooked pork. For the first time, three
generations prepare the *blutwurst*: Mother and
daughter trim fat and dice, while Oma wobbles
to the sink to wash casings inside and out,
the language between them mostly gesture.
The girl is afraid of her grandmother, though
Oma pulls her little brother down the street
almost every morning in her squeaking

cart, stopping to chatter while the boy holds
his stuffed bear out to the neighborhood
women. Now, as first sun knifes through
calico curtains, watching her grandmother
furiously work she realizes that Oma really
did bend to dig seed potatoes in the old country
the day her mother was born, that she did
indeed, lifting her skirt in an oak grove that

bordered the field, squat to foal on a bed
of leaves, just the way her mother had
told her. Outside, a peddler shouts from
his horse cart, "Waddy-mel-ones," with an
unbridled intensity that pulls children from
their houses, waving pennies at him. As she
cuts on, her legs feel heavy and plodding; in
the feedbag, she imagines, a ration of words.

The Chicago Daily Blues

CHAD PREVOST

At the Empty Bottle, the acid jazz band casts out a line with a seventh,
some xylophones, drums and keyboards, hooks you in close,
then lets go. A silent movie plays against the wall: a seat, people
on and off the endless L. The lights dim and everyone stares
at the glow-in-the-dark stars. The bars on Wabash open late
and shut down early, and sometimes the best jazz is the restless sax
rising beneath you on the cross-sectioned, iron-girded underpass.
Grant Green called it the Iron City, but said a Chicago April
was like stepping into a dream. Would you be shocked if I said
they call it the Windy City because of the politicians' lies?
When I lived here the Cubs were still lovable losers, Pluto
was a planet, and I was so in love with the romance of Chicago,
I asked you to spend your life with me. Even the South Side
projects were limned in dreams, even Jimmy's 400-square-foot
flat was a launch pad. Even now, on an ordinary weekday,
signature Chicago blues leaks through the windows
of Buddy Guy's Legends. Heavy thumb-picking, howling,
"Still Waiting," and "Sweet Home Chicago," making the pain
hurt so much you can taste it in your beer, and swooning, taste
the sweetness in the hurt. The wind, like a politician, kisses you
wet on the cheeks in the night's lake air, and you breathe in deep
with no idea where to go next, just going as far as you can,
then returning, exhaling the sweet city, where I wait like a drone
for my wandering bee to remember the honeycomb, the Lydian
mode's arpeggiated pull, hitting the root tones slow and easy,
giving plenty of time between the beats for some Soul to fill in
between the stair-flights, the tracks, the cracks beneath
your feet, between you and your friends, and the stars' terrible
distance. The theme is a mood-piece set on your life letting loose
before you like the Catalinas' sails on this land-locked lake
that once was an ocean, where the silt still offers brachiopods
like common jewelry, each shell an arrested universe, like now
Michigan Avenue frozen beneath a thin dust of snow. The taxis,
shoppers, dealers all mixed up in beautiful, dissonant union.

A Walk through Chicago's Loop, Winter, 2009

MARK PRUDOWSKY

It's not the north wind blowing sleet and yesterday's mild
away that stands me up in my three mile walk from the Loop,
but how all around me, I mean really, everywhere, cranes
swing through gray sky. Even now, the city, the country
toughing it out, they still plant glass and steel deep into
sandy loam, into the north bank of the river, where

not the curved glass tower, but two barges, trapped in dirty ice
busted up in yesterday's thaw, draw my eye. Or what's on them:
gantry crane, generator, two river skiffs and four large
tool-storage boxes. Or the 20 degree–cant of the one
furthest from shore—and the absence of cable or rope
to secure all that tilts. Or how the counterweights of the elevator
scabbed to the tower, rise, disappear in the fog . . . it's not

the lunch with two friends who still live here. It's that
today they have no work and we have short memories
if we have memories at all. We worked many winters,
many unheated buildings or often outside in stiff winds
off the lake. We hated the cold. We have short memories.
I can't remember who descends from the tower,
when everything rights itself or finally disappears into a cold metal flow.

Windy City

CHRISTINA PUGH

They wrote all over the rocks, the ones
who came before and come still; choicer
than graffiti, the paint cubed and letters
blocked like epitaphs: *Acid* or *small groove*
or *baby cakes.* And primary colors whet
the schools of foam the lake makes,
its mobile cursive less serene, while the city
wells above that trace of sociability—
its steeples snuffed, or nearly, in the mist:
this could have been Christminster,
or these the moral rocks Tess read
on her journey home in terrible,
delicate boots: the shores mirror us
always, but the city transpires.

Second Sister Terrorizes Second City

MAYA QUINTERO

(a)

Those finger-deep divots
in the pavement
outside the Sears Tower?
      They're mine.

32 feet per second per second
makes a dropped penny hit
like a Hercules-slammed
      sledgehammer.

My sister moans.
You're gonna kill someone.
I tell her to have a little
      faith.

(b)

Without being asked
or paid an artist's commission,
I entered my own bovine
into the Cows on Parade
exhibit back in '99.

The Limoosine.
Plant Chicowgo.
Cow Sandburg.
PiCowso.
      Those weren't mine.

I dragged my creation
off the back of my sister's Tacoma
in the dead of city dark,
onto the steps of Goose Island Brewery
(I had considered Ditka's

Hard Rock Chicago,
Harry Caray's,
and The Berghoff first).

It stood for three days
until a truck came,
three men loaded it up,
and took it God-knows-where.

Gimme Back My Moolah!!!
Across its greenback belly,
my sister's gape-eyed face.

(c)

I am afraid of clowns.
Especially Bozo,
whose red Muppet-style
hair is too demonic,
too much like Stephen King's
flame-haired Pennywise.

No wonder I sent Larry Harmon
six Gino's East pizzas
every week for a year
and stuffed bananas
into his Honda's tailpipe.

What does he expect,
lurking around on WGN
with ghost-white face paint
and a blood-red mouth like that?

(d)

First city to use the word "jazz."
First planetarium in the Western World.
First atomic reaction.
First steel-framed skyscraper.

First elevated train system.
First commercial air flight.

First city to scar my soul
with its skyline beauty,
its hog butcher heart,
its ever-shifting battle lines.

(e)

      Still,
part of what draws me
to Chicago—this land
of churrasco and sushi,
pelmeni and sweetbreads,
this land of cowpunchers
and ballplayers, freight
handlers and policemen—
is what makes me want
to flee it.

      Or stay
and snap its long,
Grendel-dark spine.

Bartman-style.

At Shedd Aquarium

ROBYN SCHIFF

Watch them be themselves
in habitats contrived
in dark rooms with openings
like televisions broadcasting
a dimension where Pigment rides
in its original body
and metaphor initiates impractical
negotiations with Size and Color
and Speed and Silence
too thoroughly forward
but to feel
the self an excess.

Fastness, I am tired of resting.
Isn't it indecisive not to be smaller
driven through waters barely perceivable
but where a wake scribbles
a line like a Chinese character
abandoning its construction box
to slip as line only
into an opening
smaller than its shoulders?

Each fin scores the air
as it opens the surface.
A sliver of a fish circles
forever that day
as if to turn something over
in its skinny head keen
to resolve a difficulty
I have.

It is an opera with a lonesome
heroine pacing revolving moors
engineered to seem panoramic.
The diva opens and closes

the tragic mouth singing
deliberate, even breaths
intuition hears.

Theater of false proportion. Theater of constellations reconfiguring. Theater
of readjusting the reception. Theater of missing appointments. Theater of
driving into the ocean with the headlights turned lowest green and the theater
of the engine shifting into oceanic-overdrive. Theater of hearing something
coming closer and theatrical fields of theater set crops. Theater of this can not
be my life, for which, it is too quiet. Theater of seeing something moving in
the one light in the distance which is darkness. Theater of stopping. Theater
of my mistake: not coming forward, going further, the something moving
in the theater of lighting in the theater of the hour between the theater of
morning and the theater of night in the theater of years in which the theater
of regret is keeping the secret theater of the revision.

      Theater of slipping between
two points in a simulated rock-mountain.

      Theater of who will not tell
casually follows.

Pigeon Lady

TERESA SCOLLON

The one on my street
has stepped out of all
the pantheons, disguised

in muted jackets and knitted
caps. She appears daily
to look after these small ones.

If I walk too close
she stops, stands motionless
as a tree, or a god. The people

from Lincoln Park push
past her, past the birds,
in search of hip vintage

and cheaper rent. See their
heels and fitted coats,
their manufactured hair.

How visible they are, how blind,
missing the tousled one
who keeps this street awash

in flutter. She pauses,
opens her bag. It's a quiet
mind that gathers grain,

that remembers the hunger
of unloved birds. The soft nut
of her face bends toward

beauty: see the pigeons,
mottled and barred, as infinitely
variable as snowflakes, strutting

and bowing on lavender feet.
circling her with a skirt
of feathers. She moves, the skirt

flames and scatters, and the air
is suddenly nerved with
a hundred small wings.

Wishbone

DON SHARE

I have a bone to pick
with whoever runs this joint.
I don't much like
being stuck out in the rain
just to feed on the occasional
vole or baby rabbit
and these wet weed-salads
confound my intestines.
A cat can't throw himself
into the Chicago River,
not even in the luscious fall.
I get yelled at in human
language every single day
for things I can't begin
to comprehend, let alone change.
But I go on cleaning myself—
why shouldn't I?—
and so I think I smell sweet,
even though I suspect otherwise.
I wouldn't harm a fly normally,
but why doesn't anybody
take care of me? How am I
supposed to know that it's Easter,
that I'm not allowed to die
in my own bed, and that neither prong
of this wishbone is meant for me?

And Still, a Bird Is in Me

VIVIAN SHIPLEY

Picasso's fifty-foot high, sixty-two ton gift to Chicago
staring straight at me, I pick the low concrete steps
where Joseph Brodsky sat with Stephen Spender

in the Richard J. Daley Civic Center. Mouths eager,
but no works of art, not made out of Corten to keep
rust from eating them, they would have ignored the night

rain, gotten up and circled Picasso's cables and plates.
First, a horse's head floating out of ribs, its mane
draping to Cleopatra's hair. Next, a woman's profile

that must have reminded Stephen of his wife, Natasha,
who surely was modeled after a bust of Nefertiti.
Rounding the sculpture, its wings lifted them to Daedalus

and Icarus in flight. Was Joseph Brodsky pulled back
to St. Petersburg, the bombs and the sirens, by steel
spreading into the coif of a nun fleeing as his mother did

entering the crypts of the Cathedral of Smolny convent?
Unlike them, I don't move. I'm afraid to interrupt
two boys riding dirt bikes onto Picasso's curved base,

three who bank skateboards to get height for a moment
away from what waits for them on earth. In the center
of the plaza, a fountain has sprays of water that form

a tunnel young girls gauntlet to see who can become
the wettest. It is not water I would mind; for September,
the day is warm. I don't want silk clinging to my thighs

or stomach like their skirts do. With eyes of a hawk,
I watch as the boys do wheelies to lure the five girls
who eye them. Understanding gravity, how it directs

my breasts, I know I can't invent a jump that will not
swing me back to pavement. Filled with a need I cannot
name, I repeat: Joseph Brodsky and Stephen Spender.

The two could not know on that night they shared
in Chicago they would die within six months of each
other. One death was not like the other. New York City.

January 28, 1996. Joseph Brodsky's heart stopped.
He was fifty-five. This number and his death bring
perspective, give this day to me. No longer caring

about underarms that sag, that can't be resurrected,
I take off my shoes, my socks and wade right into
the fountain, my hunger, a song my body cannot sing.

Huck, with Music and Guns

BARRY SILESKY

This isn't the river, pirates, night and fog, a boy cross-dressed and ready to knock on a cabin in no country we know. But are we sure? Five days overcast, the woman at the next table wants her friend to understand the way he acts isn't always his fault. He's just careless, the way men are; it's his foreign style—Spanish, North African? Can't she forgive him?

It's like the one in the bonnet who came to the cabin in the woods—the woman who lived there knew all along he was a boy. He couldn't thread a needle. She didn't know where he came from, or why. She never thought of him "that way," but he went "too far." He grabbed her breast in public as if it were a joke. She just can't take another winter here. The plane leaves early tomorrow and she isn't coming back.

The gang leaders on the other side of town say they're going to clean up the streets and make them safe. The four she saw were laughing, slouched in a convertible on a sunny day, diamonds and gold sparkling in ears as they squealed away from the light. She didn't see a gun, and she wasn't going to look.

We're all suckers for that music, guitar ringing like bells, delicate and slow; harmony so rich we can't leave. And we love the story of gang bangers converting, whether or not they do, as much as they love the attention. Eventually, though, the raft lands, the trip's over, and the rest is farce. A spot of sun washes the table. The gang bangers aren't turning in their guns, and no one's surprised.

Chicago

PATRICIA SMITH

SOUL Butcher for the Country,
      Heart Breaker, Stacker of the Deck,
      Player with Northbound Trains, the Nation's Black Beacon;
      Frigid, windy, sprawling,
      City of Cold Shoulders.

They tell me you have lied and I believe them,
for I have seen your Mississippi women stumbling
Madison Street searching for their painted city legs.

And they tell me you are evil and I answer: Yes, I know.
I have seen babies cooking their hair, fingering blades,
changing their names to symptoms of jazz.

And they speak of souls you swallow, and my reply is:
On the shadowed faces of men in the factory lines
I have witnessed the beginnings of the furthest falling.

And having answered so I turn to the people who spit at my city,
and I spit back at them before I say:

Come and show me another city with head thrown back wailing
    bladed blue, field hollers, so astounded to be breathing and bleeding.
Spewing electric hymns rhythmed against the staccato pound of
    fiery steel presses, here is a defiant ass whupper
    shaking its massive fists at sweating southern "towns";

Feral as a junkyard mutt, taut, muscled against his enemy, shrewd
    as an explorer pitted against an untried land,
        Wily as a Louisiana boy faced with days of concrete,
        Wiry-headed,
        Digging,
        Destroying,
        Deciding,
        Swallowing, expelling, swallowing,

Under the rubble, thrusting forth, laughing with
perfect teeth,
Shedding the terrible burden of skin, laughing as a white
man laughs,
Laughing even as a soldier laughs, addicted to the need of his next battle,
Laughing and bragging that under that skin is the cage of his ribs
And under his ribs beats a whole unleashed heart.
          Laughing!
Laughing the frigid, windy, sprawling laughter of
   a southern man, folded against the cold, sparkling, sweating,
proud to be
SOUL Butcher for the Country,
      Heart Breaker, Stacker of the Deck,
      Receiver of Northbound Trains and the Nation's Black Beacon.

Meditation on a Shorewalk with Old Emil
in the "Windy City" of My Youth

DAN STRYK

I. M. Emil Stryk (1899-1995)

Teeth chatter as my soggy shoes gouge sandpocks where I'd once *strained*
to keep up with him — where I've now returned, late in my life, to peer out
toward a few brave yachtspars needling smoky light on the horizon, blurred
by my squinting tears. Face-lash of a howling wind that names Chicago's
character, hulking beneath this "concrete time" of Lake Michigan's crescent
shore . . . where the vanished Iroquois' fishing lore of *Serpents spied from
thatched pontoons*, he'd fill me with each walk, had spurred my *distant
dreaming*.

But further on that past would fade as we'd approach those heaps of refuse
quarry-rock and cast-away cement from the building sites on opposite ends of
the great half-moon of beach. *Here* where Emil talked to me, some forty years
before that *feels* like yesterday, in morning's windy sleet . . . .

When his sudden yell pierced that gusty roar, as I'd nearly slipped flatfooted
down the dripping slab of concrete sprouting iron prongs above the beating
waves (his strong hand clutching my thin shoulder bone) . . . and then he'd
told me how *he'd* fallen years before, when moving *dreamy and flatfooted, here,*
along great slabs fresh-piled from some razed factory wall.

We'd lingered on that heap above the surf, while he told me how his boot
had slid over a patch of algae-muck to flip him on his (thank God!) leather-
covered back into a pit of shards from weathered pop bottles and metal
fragments of beer cans — small inventive ingots, formed by endless beating
of those waves, I'd stuff my pockets with in "treasure-dream." Those waves
that had so deeply carved my childhood as well; and *his* own buoyant life that,
tough as hell and wise, would only lose its clarity of mind toward the end.

: : :

"Danny, you remember *this*" — he'd hunkered down to show me in that
scuffed-brown leather coat he wore, resembling a sturdy bear — "always climb
like the Indians did. Crouching close to stone, knees bent. And *always, always,
Son*, on the balls of your feet . . ."

A Sheaf for Chicago

LUCIEN STRYK

Something queer and terrifying about Chicago:
one of the strange "centres" of the earth . . .
—D. H. Lawrence to Harriet Monroe

I. Proem

Always when we speak of you, we call you
Human. You are not. Nor are you any
Of the things we say: queer, terrifying.

It is the tightness of the mind that would
Confine you. No more strange than Paris
Is gay, you exist by your own laws.

Which to the millions that call you theirs,
Suffice, serve the old gargantuan needs.
Heaped as if just risen—streaming, unsmirched—

From seethings far below, you accept all.
By land, air, sea they come, certain to find
You home. For those you've once possessed, there's no

Escaping: always revealed in small
Particulars—a bar, a corner—you
Reappear complete. Even as I address

You, seeing your vastness in alleyways
And lots that fester Woodlawn, I have
A sense of islands all around, made one

By sea—that feeds and spoils yet is a thing
Apart. You are that sea. And home: have
Stamped me yours for keeps, will claim me when,

Last chances spent, I wrap it up for good.
You are three million things, and each is true.
But always home. More so and more deeply

Than the sum of antheaps we have made of
You, reenter every night to dream you
Something stone can never be. And met

However far away, two that call you
Home, feel beyond the reach of words to tell
Like brothers who must never part again.

II. Child in the City

In a vacant lot behind a body shop,
I rooted for your heart, O city,
The truth that was a hambone in your slop.

Your revelations came as thick as bees,
With stings as smarting, wings as loud,
And I recall those towering summer days

We gathered fenders, axles, blasted hoods
To build Cockaigne and Never-never Land,
Then beat for dragons in the oily weeds.

That cindered lot and twisted auto mound,
That realm to be defended with the blood,
Became, as New Year swung around,

A scene of holocaust, where pile on pile
of Christmas trees would char the heavens
And robe us demon-wild and genie-tall

To swirl the hell of 63rd Place,
Our curses whirring by your roofs,
Our hooves a-clatter on your face.

III. The Balloon
(To Auguste Piccard, his day at Soldier Field)

As you readied the balloon, tugging
At the ropes, I grabbed my father's hand.
Around us in stone tiers the others

Began to hold their breath. I watched my
Father mostly, thinking him very
Brave for toying with his pipe. Then when

You filled the giant sack with heated
Air and, waving, climbed into the
Gondola with a bunch of roses

Thrust at you, I freed my hand, cheered
And started clapping. I caught your eye,
You smiled, then left the ground. The people

Filed for exits when, twisting in
The wind, you veered above the lake, a
Pin against a thundercloud. But I

Refused to budge. My father stooped to
Beat me and cracked his precious briar
On the stone. And still I wouldn't leave.

He called me a young fool and dragged me,
Bawling, to the streetcar. But I couldn't
Stop watching you. I stayed up all that night,

Soaring ever higher on your star,
Through tunneled clouds and air so blue
I saw blue spots for hours. In the morning

My father laughed and said you came back down.
I didn't believe him then, and never will.
I told him I was glad he broke his pipe.

IV. The Beach

Even the lake repulses:
I watch them where, shellacked
      And steaming

In barbaric light, they
Huddle in their shame, the maids
      And busboys.

Even the lovers dare not
Step where the goddess rose in
      Tinted foam,

But paw each other, gape,
Spin radio dials. And hulking
      Over cards

Mothers whip strings of
Curse like lariats, jerking
      The children

From the shore when, suddenly
Across the beach, they hear:
      "Lost! Child lost!"

None rise. The breakers drown
Voices, radios; peak white, pound
      In like fists.

V. Mestrovic's Indians
(*Equestrian statues, Michigan Avenue*)

With bare heels sharp as spurs
They kick the bronze flanks of
      The horses.

But what sane beast would brave
A river wild as this, choked
      As it is

With jagged tin and all
That snarling rubber? and
      Ford to where?

Along the other bank, while the
Great arms pointing with their
      Manes convulse

In anger, the merchants
Dangle strings of gewgaws
      In the sun.

But no mere hoof was meant
For plunging here, and why, the
      Horses seem

To ask, would even redskins
Climb a shore where not one
      Grassblade springs?

VI. City of the Wind

All night long the lake-blast
      Rattled bones of
Dreamers in that place of glass.

Awake, they heard a roaring
      Down the lots and
Alleyways where wind flung

Rainspout, fencepost, toolshed,
      As if the town
Were tossing on the flood

Of space. All night, it seemed,
      A horde of giants
Came trampling overhead,

Tore limbs, wrenched screens, spilled
        Glass like chips of
Sky. Next day through, the dazed

Ones rooted in the mire,
        Then, back in beds,
Dreamt the city fairer

Than before. But how,
        Snapped antennae
Pulling roofs askew,

Autos tipped hub-deep in silt,
        Could dream raise up
What dream alone had built?

VII. Eve

        In Calcutta, I found her in a stall,
                A thing for sale,
Breasts like burnished gourds: some things one does not buy.

        In Isfahan her eyes were black as wells
                Entreating alms
Of all who passed: there are deserving charities.

        In Amsterdam above a darkened street
                A bay window
Framed her sundries, proffering bliss: I was not sold.

        In Seville she wore a gypsy shawl and
                Bangles on her
Dancing feet: the silver dropped around them was not mine.

        In Paris she hugged me down the avenue,
                Skirt a jocund
Sail, towed by the dollars in my purse: I tacked for home.

In Chicago she waits behind a door
          No common key
Can budge: who enters there will never get away.

VIII. The Gang

One can hardly extricate them
From the props they lounge against,
Or see them for the smoke lips

Link in chains that will not hold.
At night the sound of pennies tossed
Upon the sidewalk-cracks is like

A slowly breaking mirror
Which reflects the little that they
Are. What girl dare pass and not

Be whistled at? Their appraisements
Are quick, absolute: that water
Freezes into ice needs scant

Deliberation. Whatever
The day sweeps up, their sole
Antagonist is boredom, which

By merely standing around, they
Thwart at every turn but one.
They scorn whom others envy,

The man who ambles by, duty
Snapping at the heels, and should lovers
Cross, there is a sudden flinging down

(By eyes so starved, they almost moan)
And then a coupling in the dust.
Allow them such years to lean

And wait. Soon they must approach
The selfsame corner, and hail
The gang that is no longer there.

IX. The Neighborhood

Long away, I find it pure
Exotic; no matter that they roll
The sidewalks up at ten and boys

Want height to leap for basketballs:
It is a place, and there are corners
Where one does what one would do.

Come back, I find the expected
Changes: shabby streets grown shabbier,
The mob all scattered, old girl friends

Losing more of what's been lost,
The supermarts turned up like sows
To give the brood of grunters suck,

And Mother, like a thickening tree
Whose roots work deeper as the woodsman
Nears, spread over all, the wind which sweeps

Across her whispering "Stay on."
Two weeks of that, and there are
Other whispers that I heed.

The train pulls in and I descend,
To mount before it pulls away.
Goodbye, Mother, goodbye! I'm off

Again to Someplace Else, where
Chafing together once a month
The strangers sit and write sweet letters home.

Wall Painting in Chicago Bar: "Richard J. Daley, Mayor"

RICHARD TERRILL

It's three blocks from where my Cantonese in-laws live since they moved out
of Chinatown. Bridgeport, so-called: no bridge, no port, but working class. I'd
thought the neighborhood tough—afraid to go out, lock your door at night.
But one couple on the corner stools, who could be Torres or Rodriguez, toasts
me with pints of MGD, while guys with broad faces of Poles wear White Sox
caps and watch Notre Dame football on the one working TV. A mixed race
couple plays chess near the back exit, its locked door and sign that reads: *Must
Remain Open During Business Hours.*

When my stepsons, young men now, invited me to go shoot pool, I said,
"What?" thinking I'd misunderstood. Thanksgiving night, snow in the air
but not on the ground, all three of us refugees from cousins, uncles, and Mom
(aka my wife), we're visiting from out of town, shooting against a couple guys
named Vito and Cesar who belong to this parish, orderlies at the hospital we
walked past to get to the bar. Crucifixes dangle from their necks as they eye
the corner pocket.

Notre Dame goes ahead by a touchdown ("They'll lose," Vito says, not looking
up from his shot).

Leftover turkey cools throughout the neighborhood, and we're warming up
in the neon beer sign light. The balls rattle alive when Vito breaks, explode
like neutrons, but nothing drops. The older patrons have these days off work.
Some argue about bowl picks and the Bears; the young buzz on cell phones,
like my sons: *Are you there? Are you in Texas? No, dude, I'm in Chicago, shooting
pool and doing shots.*

Richard J. Daley's beneficent gaze softens the cone of light above the pool
table, Mayor Daley the first, in his black suit and red tie. The white below
the iris in each eye gives him a hound-like steadfastness. He's dogged for the
contentment of his ward. Like Mary (aka the Virgin Mother) he looks skyward
for bliss, and perhaps for votes, keeping watch over the neighborhood, over
Vito, Cesar, the bartender, and us, as Southern Cal threatens to score.

"Completed in '53, retouched 2000," the inscription below the portrait reads."
The year I was born and the year I realized I was as happy as I'm likely to get,

unretouched and unrevisited. For this is Bridgeport, no bridge in sight, no port of call for any ship. We're on the green felt sea, on the exit ramp of life, we older patrons, the evening of this holiday my in-laws don't celebrate—rice, curried lamb, and bean curd sheets for our turkey day repast. But I'm not Cantonese, not ethnic working class, not Hispanic and sitting at the corner stool. There are a lot of things I'm not, here without my wife (aka all that I have in this flat world), with my grown sons and the good shots they leave the other guys.

Notre Dame scores again as time runs out. I'm going to bank the six off the rail and set up the eight in the side.

In the Intersection, Jackson and State

TONY TRIGILIO

Without looking, I could cross Jackson
without getting struck, guided by voices, a hum
of tires on coarse pavement. I want to scale
one of those slopes, the blushed steel
of the CNA Building, grab the Monadnock's
frayed terra cotta drapery and climb.

Lakeside wind so loud it changes the subject.
In dreams, I lie too long on spring grass, pikes
still dead despite thaw. Ants crawl my arms,
bees swarm. Nature an antique, an abandoned
oak table behind glass, waiting for me
to test its legs, barter a price.

I'm afraid of nature. Orange, Brown Line
trains cross paths, the distant touch of negotiators.
Rivers changing course, office windows bound in mist.
Pavement accumulates, dismantles, rises; an array of noise
come again. One block east, a construction crew
is drilling, their hammers lift from State like smoke.

Tourists and Bum, Art Institute of Chicago

ALPAY ULKU

That bum likes to say that he provides a valid service, that he earns a living as an entertainer, but he's just a bum. He's careful to say *help the homeless*, careful not to claim he's homeless himself. He hustles though, and he's not stupid. He announces that Route 66 begins beneath at his feet, which is true. And thus begins the spiel, on and on. A dollar here, a couple there. He works the crowd while they cross the street, skips ahead and comes back, *hey skipeedee do* that street is wide, the traffic lights are long. He works the crowd that's waiting at the curb, stranded there. A group from Oklahoma U seems amused, some are smirking, a few among them glare. The bum is black, the tourists, the ones who give him money, are almost always white. It's an easy feel-good, and the price is right. That money adds up fast.

Run for Your Life

JUDITH VALENTE

            Is it true some people
can foresee their own death? Like John F. Kennedy
    peering into that open-roof limousine
from the top floor of a Hilton months before Oswald,
    saying *Somebody could really get you.*
Or Private William L. Lynn at 15, writing home
    from San Diego, *Oh Mom hurry. Soon as possible*
if you can. Try to get me out by Sunday. Bring some clothes
    when you come, and three months later, trudging
through the Bataan peninsula, a bullet sails through his neck.

            Today, walking
to mail some packages, I spot a crowd
    gazing up at an office tower, and a man says
a window fell from the 29th floor
    of the CNA Insurance Building, sliced through
a woman's head while she was walking with her daughter.
    That's what came out of her. He points
to a puddle of something brown, red and gray
    lying in front of the PMI Parking lot:
blood, skin and brain tissue like rain-soaked Kleenex.
    The blood dark like car oil, already drying.

            Picture that woman
who took the bus or train downtown. One minute
    she's walking along Wabash Avenue,
holding her little girl's hand. The next, she's barreling
    through the after-life. *As unpredictable a death*
as exists, a friend of mine says later. This strikes me
    because just last week I was reading W. S. Merwin's
"For the Anniversary of My Death" where he says
    every year without knowing it, we pass
the date of our death. Now passersby gesture
    toward the CNA building as if to say,

That's the one, there's the perpetrator,
half expecting the police—who have whisked away
    the child and thrown up yellow cordons—
to slap handcuffs around the CNA, its pink frame
    always calling attention to itself. Now every building
beats with the heart of a potential murderer,
    though the Beaux Arts buildings cut a *bella figura,*
look less suspect than the Art Deco ones.
    Only the wrought-iron facade of Carson Pirie Scott
inspires trust: an English gentleman
    with gapped teeth in black tie, tails.

        I imagine
that woman's name, though no one knows it yet,
    how perhaps she went to Mass on Sundays,
cooked with cumin and cilantro, felt bored
    by the smell of her own bed sheets. How she
probably has a husband at work somewhere
    at a Boudin's bakery or Chevy dealership,
(though tomorrow the papers will say she was
    Anna Flores, 36, of South Spaulding Avenue,
downtown to pick up a job application). And I hope
    her little girl is young enough for the mind
to toss a black veil over this afternoon,

        like John F. Kennedy Jr.
saying he remembered nothing of his father's funeral
    though it took place the day he turned three.
I think of the ways I've worried death could
    catch me, like stumbling into a gunfight
some Friday at the Mid-City National Bank,
    or an aneurysm: exploding firecracker in the brain.
Hoping death wouldn't just show up at my door,
    a discourteous guest, but drop a note in the mail,
say months, years in advance,

        as polite company would do,
so I'd have time to imitate Ben Gazzara
    in *Run for Your Life,* travel to a new city

each week helping complete strangers
    find their passion in life. Time to tear up my journals,
press the clothes in the laundry basket,
    finish the crossword puzzles on my nightstand,
toss out my torn underpants and apologize for decades
    of bad behavior before removing the robe of life,
folding it neatly, not letting it fall.

Adagio Villanelle

MARTHA MODENA VERTREACE-DOODY

When red lights lower crossing gates, you turn
on Ogden, leave me at a corner café where
sunrise brings shadows of wind-blown grass

to the window, my coffee, your newspaper—
its five-line filler circled: an African lion,
head lowered in red morning light, crosses

the foot of Cold Knob Mountain. Maned.
A four-foot tail. A bow hunter aims
at sunrise shadows. Wind-blown grass

hides bait: pounds of raw chicken.
The lion long gone. Bartok's *Adagio*
trickles down my back—red lights lowered

in his "unspeakable grief." The hunter's bane:
whatever it takes to lose café doors
to sunrise, shadows, wind-blown grass.

Late morning. I drain my cup,
greet the swell of your roar with no surprise
when red lights lower crossing gates. You turn
sunrise into shadows of wind-blown grass.

Nighthawks Transfixed

GALE RENEE WALDEN

It's only the glass bending inward and the solid alone of "Man in Fedora Drinking Coffee,"
which makes you return again and again. A light exactly blinding.

Outside, reflected, the shadow etches into itself
changes dimensions, makes you say *meaning*.

Inside, behind the counter, the hash cook is redefining art—
not the form of the self curving but more the slant of the ordinary—
salt, pepper, the catsup bottle unturned.

Even as it diminished (not everyone is so lucky) the shadow looms
in imagination and—abracadabra—manifests: A couple at a counter with Solitude

A telescope. *Happy. Happy. Happy. Daylight over the river*
A single chord rising. Then pianos. The jag of her smile.
"Say maybe he loved her." "Well maybe he did."

Haven't you been taught all along that the clock,
when thrown from a train, is silenced?
The train disappears blinking into the night only to reemerge
on a museum wall where the absence of clocks is always significant.

Deceptive, isn't it? This, which poses as past, which poses as art,
a slight hiccup in time into a world where Bogart is taking a non-cancerous drag
"How could we not have known?" the voice ticks again and again,
an off-beat more gently, "How could we have known?"

On the magnificence of deserted city streets: a saxophone,
one patent leather shoe tapping on aluminum

Inheritance

NICOLE WALKER

They didn't tell me, when I moved to Phoenix,
that I'd have to bring my own water.
That was okay, of course, since I'd been born in Chicago
and had the entire Lake Michigan at my disposal.
My parents still live in a hut
in Saugatuck. I ask them to send my share
of the Great Lake, my birthright,
in individual plastic bottles.
It comes by train. My wrist is sore
from cap-twisting and though I only take
sips, the ounces last for barely an hour.
Some days even I—
as I lie in February, under my blossoming
bougainvillea, listening to the freeway
moan along without me—
dream of the lake's sandy beaches
that take up the even snow.
With Gary, Indiana to my back,
Milwaukee, Wisconsin to my front,
the white smoothes me plain.
The snow snows there in three full
states, maybe more. The snow has flattened my
Chicago like it flattened the whole
Midwest but thanks to that one-note
frozen landscape, I reach across whole
states and across them my visibly wet breath.

Cloud Gate

ELLEN WEHLE

Millennium Park

Because no man doesn't love to drink of his own image,

I dominate the plaza.

Think hot silver: Electric filament.

Mercury bead. Solder spark. Light inside a glacier.

Vapor fogged on photographic plates.

Or that fish who slumbers, beatific, all winter at lake-bottom,

Kindling clouds out of empty

Mind and air. *If this is the only way in . . .*

If I am . . . in fact . . . sky's foyer.

The Facts as I Know Them

SCOTT WIGGERMAN

Somewhere between Germany and Chicago,
Joseph Wiggermann lost an "n" at the end of his name.
But along the way he found a wife, Caroline Spauer,
and by 1884 they married, their traveling
thereafter confined to the edges of DuPage County.
Joseph was a blacksmith, a wheelwright,
a career well suited to an immigrant with limited English,
decent enough to provide for Caroline and the seven children,
six when Dominick succumbed in infancy to flu.
Caroline herself died eleven days short of forty-eight,
washing, cleaning, cooking, a workhorse to the end.
Ferdinand, the baby of the family, called Fred,
would become my father's father in 1934.

The Great Famine's shadow still lurked over Ireland
in the 1890s when Thomas McShea courted Catherine Ring.
Leaving the rocky glens of County Cork,
the McSheas sailed for what was still called the New Land
in a turn-of-the-century wave of Irish immigration.
They made their way, like the Wiggermanns before them,
to the city of Chicago, as good a place as any to be Irish.
Like many of his countrymen, Thomas joined the police,
but short of forty was shot in the line of duty,
the year before Capone moved to town,
ushering in a whole new era of gangster violence.
Thomas left behind his wife and three children,
Thomas, Jr., Vern, and little emerald-eyed Catherine,
who would become my father's mother in 1934.

For if I don't write it down, even less will remain.

Blueaille

KATHERINE WILLIAMS

The Joseph Cornell collection at the Art Institute of Chicago

libretti   blue marbles   ticket stubs
Here is how to get anhingas into the shabby
seaside lodgings of your untravelled memories:
in their cages fashion operettas of the mundane.
balsa wood   ceramic actresses   indigo silk
Of the life devoted to an invalid brother,
make you a life of Ten Thousand Exquisite Things.
Be the Ulysses of the tethered ankle.
cat bones   lithographs of female children
The nights of your grimy little street will be
cerulean nights of wild auroras, and its days,
days of starlight eclipsing sunshine.
mirrors   menus sent by admirers   clocksprings
Your room will be the artfullest nook
on the Seine, your guests the great
physicists and ballerinas of Europe.
wood spheres   goblets   lenses   DC circuitry
Let others found their dynasties, paint portraits
in lapis: yours will be the seed
that falls on the bluest peninsula.
corks   exploded dovecotes   mouse fuzz
We can almost hear the tiny marimba of a music
box, pop and hiss of vinyl enshrining
a tenor in a cobalt enamel gramophone.
clay bubble-pipes   piston rings   feathers
When the rest of us crowd before your
impeccably dilapidated steamer trunk
blue light shall emanate as it is opened.
Blueaille, you called it.

Fields

MARTIN WILLITTS, JR.

Chicago is a hemorrhaging city
whose angels left molten steel factories
for the pasteurized outskirts, their arms weighted down
with Blues from Paul Butterfield's harmonica, shifting
as railroad cars switching political allegiances
depending on the ward bosses, carrying problems
on their wide shoulders long as regret
on the overshadowed shorelines of Lake Michigan

the steel mills closed a long time ago,
like everywhere all at once around the country,
only here sparks still splash upwards
into new galaxies, past slaughterhouses silent as whorehouses
when prohibition stopped raising a small slot above the door
to hear the password slip in, a gat under the arm for assurances

so many things left, packing their suitcases with streetlights,
and they are not going to return any time soon

for this too, is Chicago, a place that cannot be laid low
from a sucker's punch, or razed by the Great 1871 fire
purging sinners and saints alike, not owned by Capone
finally machine gunning the competition
before the IRS and syphilis got him,

Chicago has seen them come and go with a long eye towards
failure and success, the 1940 Blacks leaving sharecropping
for the outgrowth of ghettos and those that followed
found even less scraps, that when there is growth and opportunity
it is a bitter prostitute shrinking and wrinkling with overuse

that too is Chicago, the moneymakers losing only so much money
to political graft that can line only so many pockets
while things flow backwards like the Chicago River

the Loop can connect only so much before it loses it all,
elevating people above the city like angels of rust
while below the Marshall Field & Company clock
the dissolute move shadows on State Street,

I carried my high school art aspirations to the Art Institute,
waited my anxious turn among the fidgety, an immigrant
moving into new places, feeling overwhelmed by its size,
my artwork folded like prayer hands in a brown folio,
saw the competition drawings, withdrawing before certain rejection

I had come to Chicago like so many before me and left in the rush
of crowds coming towards Chicago, my failure delivered
sure as traffic is delivered from salvation as it passes endless
as days on the Eisenhower Expressway under the US Post Office

reflected on my face, on the freshly washed windows,
was the man behind me wearing a Cubs hat, eternally optimistic,
glistening as a rubbed Buddha.

At the Library

JANET WONDRA

Roosevelt University's Auditorium Building,
designed by Louis Sullivan and Dankmar Adler

Under the high barreled ceiling
I expand. Suddenly
things seem possible, as they should
in college. Space, volume
to breathe, to make sweeping gestures,
construct in imagination the perfect
anything: the small, safe, non-polluting car,
the personal aircraft whose mother is a dragonfly,
the gathering where at last the bigwigs
see that killing young soldiers and families walking
to market is an act that replicates for generations.
And you elaborate the dream beyond
what Miss America might say,
you see so clearly now in this grand space.

As you walk into the stacks,
isn't it like the mind itself, row after row,
multi-leveled, multi-volumed, a little musty?
Just as you fear the book you must
have, the one to clarify everything,
is checked out, mis-shelved, lost forever,
there it is, waiting, a patient animal, and in it you see
what you hoped for—more—like double doors
thrown open before you, room after room
in a welcoming mansion. You carry your book out

into the open air where the heaviness of the tables
reminds you your work is serious.
Each table bears its green banker's lamp,
the light like the slow dawn
of understanding. The windows fly open
to the lake, moody as a teenager,
but often its blue-green sweep

is so large, jeweled, you want to do
something, make something,
since you can't gather its expanse into your arms.
The flag tosses, its hardware
clanking against the pole in maritime fashion.
Buckingham Fountain pushes vertical,
impossibly high and plumed, then sinks
to the pretensions of an everyday
waterspout. Isn't that like your faith
in yourself, vertical ebb and flow?

All this I want for my students:
grandiose dreams, which scaled down
take on a practical purity,
concentrated knowledge, history
bound in covers bearing the patina
of other hands. The darkness
of the walnut tables mirrors the night
resolving over the lake, a photograph
in its chemical bath traveling backwards;
then dawn
as if stage lights are slowly coming up
on a production you don't yet know
will shine in your eye forever.
Stepping into the library, I awaken,
walk into wonder as if willingly
stepping out on a limb, brave
as a bird, ignorant of aerodynamics
yet still, willing to fly.

Chicago Chronicle

STEPHEN CALDWELL WRIGHT

Not many talk much of the clouds
Way up, over Chicago,
Though they are plentiful too,
Thickly flurried, dispassionate
In the breaking banks of shapings
Less than familiar to flying metal—
Searing wings, droning through the air,
Slicing astronomical shallowness.

Not too many know much
About the little big things
Like Lucile's Cafe on the corner
Of Cicero and some Other Avenue,
Nor do they remember the olde
Cylindrical smokies of McCormick's;
The Brass and Opal Days of the Blackstone,
Nor the spiraling smaller, swifter, dimmer lanes
Of a younger, more innocent-of-its-reaches Lake Shore Drive.

Not many remember the trestle, the stables, the bargain bay;
Only a few see the city of the "Hawk" in the Eagle's sway.

Chicago,

BRENDA YATES

on Monday, you were beautiful. Summer, yet low humidity, pleasant
temperature & light breezes. En route from the airport, even the Field
bustled in a city-ness living & working close. Under 90-foot ceilings,
Sue, famous Tyrannosaurus (largest, most complete ever found), put
us & our tiny voices in perspective. Sweeping marble stairs, columns,
balconies, palatial hall—fitting for a cathedral/temple/church/mosque
of natural history, of cultures now disappeared or disappearing into its
sacred vault-rooms.

Let us mourn ourselves; celebrate ourselves; let us be horrified by ourselves &
yes, glory in ourselves. Here is a place to contemplate what we've allowed to
happen, what we've made happen, what has happened to us. Look at what
we built, at what we destroyed.

Later, in the suburban backyard of a 1930s art deco house (scratch a
Chicagoan to find date, style & probably architect of most any structure),
we sit under Siberian oaks, soothed by Rose of Sharon blooms, wine &
conversation—as cardinals, robins, finches, settle in to wait for dawn, as
chipmunks slip back to night ground, as throbbing waves of cicada song
rise & fall into the darkening air.

Let us lay ourselves down to dream of flatlands, leafy & grassy, beside an
ever-present lake, lullabyed by night creatures secure enough to sing.

Chicago, Tuesday is coffee on the sun porch, summer dew on lawns—
another temperate, island-paradise day. Train stations like a sweet idea
of how public transportation could work (after all we're from LA). Clean,
quiet double-deckers whisk us through railroad yards & neighborhoods
of an older city as cheerful conductors walk the aisles punching tickets,
like something out of a movie. We disembark, board the short-lived
seasonal indulgence of water-taxi & ferry.

The river, we're often told, flows in the opposite direction from what it
once did, thanks to city fathers & engineers who saw that waste could
be controlled only if not dumped into the lake. We float downstream,
along the banks of America's history. Here stood the first fort, first

trading post, the wharves, docks, railroad depot, the barn where Mrs. O'Leary's cow may or may not have kicked over the lantern that caused the great conflagration which . . . rebuilt the city. Architects came like meadow grass to burned-over forest & kept coming. Each built new, then new over old, over merely new, in air rights over railroads, up against/ in context with massive brick warehouse; low, earth-bound sprawl of commerce; tall, pointy, civic gothic; European ornate; prairie style; modern; art deco; new art deco; retro; postmodern; post-postmodern. Angled, square, more rectangular, tall & needle-narrow, wedding-cake stack, oval, circle, spiral. The corner-loving teacher who never spoke again to a student committing the heresy of round. My neck hurts from looking up.

Let us pay homage to these shrines of the imagination & notice when crickets join the chorus. Country has come to city.

Chicago, Wednesday you are morning of light rain & sticky air that blows away. We wander miles of man-made hills that recreate midwestern prairies before settlements, forts, trappers or city dwellers. How many, how different the landscapes were. Dry slope, wetland, stream bank, fen, or graveled mounds glaciers left. Sunflowers & grasses grow higher than our heads; there's thistle, clover, milkweed, then marsh, pond, creek & flocks of tiny birds, goldfinches, ducks, swans, meadowlarks & unidentifiable loners. Butter- or may- or dragon- or damsel-flies, grasshoppers that hop as well as fly, loud buzz of June-bugs & the unseen. Turtles plop & swim, rabbits jump-dart, mice rustle underbrush & in the distance, tall white poplars are turning the undersides of their leaves into the wind until they shine like silver coins.

Supper by candlelight on the patio; poems with wine.

Let us remember what provides. Let us renew the pleasure of understanding something not of ourselves in ourselves, the magic that is art. Tonight, let us listen as the voices of birds add themselves to the choir, like poets, singing us to sleep.

Chicago, it's Thursday; I begin to think that you are always beautiful. We walk your parks, under the meeting-place "bean" & flying wings of Gehry's open-air concert hall. We walk over bridges, down to the river, up again. We walk by towers where waterfalls pour down & rainbow, where fountains spout from mouths of faces projected on walls as shrieking children drench themselves in the spray. We walk to Picasso's horse where children climb &

slide down massive metal plates. We walk into buildings, through lobbies, past paintings, on grand staircases & mosaic tiles with surprise after surprise of color & design. We stand under a stained-glass dome that sheds holy light over all visitors. We walk to the Art Institute for lunch & reunion of Michael's Peace Corps group from Chile, before Pinochet. Laughter & pictures of fresh-faced kids, bright eyes, thick, glossy hair, looking as if they were fourteen. Here was the school we built . . . the one-room house we lived in—no heat, electricity, or running water. Remember . . . how cold it got . . . chamber pots . . . gravity showers . . . candles . . . the kerosene lamps . . . guitars & songs . . . bottles of Pisco & cheap wine . . .

Here's the old pickup we traveled in to see Bobby Kennedy when he came. Here are . . . the people who took us in when our roof blew off & the animals they raised, the gardens they tended & the life they led, trying, like us to do good at an impossible time, in an impossible place in that impossible world.

Let us remember the part of ourselves that still wants that, yet recognize how arrogant it was to think we could. Let us remember how much we still need to try, how foreign our selves would be to us if we didn't.

Dinner in the neighborhood café is Jim's funny tales of farm, of gridiron, of Harvard Law—all of us telling stories of here, there & everywhere, the way you might come into a small town where time has not yet imposed its orderly narrative.

Let us be grateful for friends who know us & for nights like this—when fog rolls in, when heavy air comes over the lake oiling the waves, dampening the high end of night choir, deepening the sound as though the veritable ground had opened its mouth to join the singing.

Chicago, Friday is goodbye. Pat tells Michael he's been seduced: in summer, Chicago is the beautiful woman you wine, dine & flirt with, have a great time with. In winter you take her home; she takes off her makeup, removes her wig, her elegant clothes & takes out her teeth. It's only then you know Chicago.

Goodbye cardinals & robins, coffee in the garden. Goodbye ever-present lake. Goodbye river whose course has been altered & changed from toxic to merely dangerous. Goodbye ever-changing city. Goodbye youth revisited. Goodbye Pat & Jim & Ginny & Tom. Goodbye us—there & then, here & now & again.

Contributors' Notes

Kathryn Almy grew up in the southwest suburbs of Chicago. She is now a freelance writer living in Kalamazoo, Michigan. Her poems have been published in *Willow Review, shady side review, All Poetry Is Prayer: A Fire Anthology,* and *Lansing Online News.* Her included poem was inspired by Terrance Hayes's poem "Root."

Nin Andrews is the author of several books of poetry and short fiction. Her most recent collection, *Southern Comfort,* was published in 2010.

Dori Appel is the author of a collection of poems, *Another Rude Awakening* (2008). Her poems have also been widely published in magazines and anthologies. A playwright as well as a poet, she was the winner of the Oregon Book Award in Drama in 1998, 1999, and 2001.

Cristin O'Keefe Aptowicz is the author of five books of poetry, most recently *Everything Is Everything* (2010), as well as the author of the canonical poetry slam history book, *Words in Your Face: A Guided Tour through Twenty Years of the New York City Poetry Slam* (2008). Aptowicz most recently served as the 2010–2011 ArtsEdge Writer-in-Residence at the University of Pennsylvania and was additionally awarded a 2011 National Endowment for the Arts Fellowship in Poetry. www.aptowicz.com.

Rane Arroyo was a professor of English and creative writing at the University of Toledo. His poetry has appeared in the *Massachusetts Review,* the *Hawaii Review, Hotel Amerika,* and *Prairie Schooner.* He died of a cerebral hemorrhage in May 2011. The last words from his final poetry reading at SUNY/Brockport were "Live. Then Write."

Michael Austin's articles and essays have appeared in *Esquire, GQ, Outside,* and the *Chicago Tribune Magazine.* The wine columnist for the *Chicago Sun-Times,* he is also a faculty member of the Old Town School of Folk Music, where he teaches bodhran. This is his first published poem.

Marvin Bell lived in old Hyde Park, Chicago, prior to urban renewal, first at 51st and Blackstone and later at 52nd and Kenwood. The most recent of his books are *Vertigo: The Living Dead Man Poems* and *Whiteout,* a collaboration with photographer Nathan Lyons.

Mary Grace Bertulfo is a Chicago-based wordsmith who writes fiction, essays, features, and profiles about her twin passions: nature and Filipino culture. She's written for CBS, Schlessinger video productions, *Sierra Magazine*, and *Chicago Wilderness Magazine* among others. Currently, Mary Grace is at work on a babaylan-inspired historical novel set in the Philippines. www.mgbertulfo.com.

Allen Braden is the author of *A Wreath of Down and Drops of Blood* and was poet-in-residence for the Poetry Center and the School of the Art Institute of Chicago in 2006.

John Bradley is the author of *You Don't Know What You Don't Know* and *Terrestrial Music* and the editor of *Eating the Pure Light: Homage to Thomas McGrath*. He teaches at Northern Illinois University.

Raised in Michigan but now living in Southern California, **John F. Buckley and Martin Ott** began their ongoing games of poetic volleyball in the spring of 2009. Poetry from their collaboration has been accepted by the *Bryant Literary Review, Center, Compass Rose, Conceit Magazine, Confrontation, Connecticut River Review, Eleven Eleven*, and *Splash of Red*.

Melisa Cahnmann-Taylor is an associate professor in language and literacy education at the University of Georgia. She has published poems and reviews in journals such as *APR, Quarterly West, Puerto del Sol, Barrow Street, Women's Review of Books, Cream City Review*, the *Georgia Review*, and *Literary Mama*. She is the winner of several Dorothy Sargent Rosenberg Prizes and a Leeway Poetry Grant and has coauthored two books, *Teachers Act Up!: Creating Multicultural Learning Communities through Theatre* (2010) and *Arts-Based Research in Education: Foundations for Practice* (2008).

Karen Carcia's poems have appeared in *Absent, Born Magazine, Conduit, Diagram, Field, Hunger Mountain*, and *Salt Hill Journal*. She is a research assistant at the University of Iowa Center for the Book and author of *On Subjects of Which We Know Nothing*.

James E. Cherry is the author of four books: *Bending the Blues*, a poetry chapbook (2003), *Shadow of Light*, a novel (2008), and *Honoring the Ancestors*, a collection of poetry nominated for a 2009 NAACP Image Award. His collection of short fiction, *Still A Man and Other Stories*, was published in 2011. He is currently an M.F.A. candidate at the University of Texas at El Paso. http://jamesecherry.com.

Susan Deer Cloud is a widely published Métis Catskill Indian, who has received various awards and fellowships, including a National Endowment for the Arts Literature Fellowship and a New York State Foundation for the Arts Fellowship. Some of her recent books are *Car Stealer, Braiding Starlight*, and *Borscht Belt Indian*. She thinks Chicago is pretty cool (which says a lot . . . coming from an obnoxious New Yorker and a tomahawk-tossing Iroquois, at that).

James Conroy has appeared in more than a hundred notable literary magazines and journals, both in the United States and abroad. He has published a poetry collection and four novels, with two new novels slated for publication in 2012. Conroy and his wife, Helen, divide their time now between Chicago, New York, and Newport, Rhode Island.

Timothy Cook was born and raised on the North Side of Chicago. He graduated from Loyola University with a B.A. in philosophy and from the M.F.A. Program for Writers at Warren Wilson College; he has received a grant from the Mookie Jam Foundation.

At home on both page and stage, **Nina Corwin** is the author of two books of poetry, *The Uncertainty of Maps* (2011) and *Conversations with Friendly Demons and Tainted Saints* (1999). She is an advisory editor for *Fifth Wednesday Journal* and curator for Chicago's Woman Made Gallery where she coedited the anthology *Inhabiting the Body: A Collection of Poetry and Art by Women*. In daylight hours, she is a practicing psychotherapist known for her work on behalf of victims of violence.

Curtis L. Crisler's books are *Pulling Scabs, Tough Boy Sonatas, Dreamist: a mixed genre novel*, and the award-winning chapbook, *Spill*. He's been published in many magazines and journals. He is an assistant professor of English at Indiana University–Purdue University Fort Wayne and a Cave Canem Fellow.

Mary Cross's poems, short stories, and essays have appeared in various journals, including *Other Voices*, the *Sun, Crazyhorse, Hotel Amerika*, Featherproof Press minibook series, and have aired on Chicago Public Radio. She has published a poetry collection *Rooms, Which Were People*. She teaches in the M.F.A. in Writing Program at the School of the Art Institute of Chicago and is currently at work on a photography project depicting horses in rescue and sanctuary environments.

James D'Agostino is the author of *Nude With Anything* (2006). His work has appeared in *Forklift, Ohio, Conduit, TriQuarterly, Third Coast, Born Magazine*, and elsewhere. He directs the B.F.A. Program in Creative Writing at Truman State University.

Stuart Dybek is the author of two books of poetry, *Streets in Their Own Ink* and *Brass Knuckles*, and three books of fiction. He is Distinguished Writer-in-Residence at Northwestern University.

Bart Edelman is a professor of English at Glendale College, where he edits *Eclipse*, a literary journal. His work has appeared in anthologies and textbooks published by City Lights Books, Etruscan Press, Harcourt Brace, Heinle, McGraw-Hill, Prentice Hall, Simon & Schuster, Thomson, University of Iowa Press, and Wadsworth. Collections of his poetry include *Crossing the Hackensack, Under Damaris' Dress, The Alphabet of Love, The Gentle Man, The Last Mojito*, and *The Geographer's Wife*.

Susan Elbe is the author of *Eden in the Rearview Mirror* and a chapbook, *Light Made from Nothing*. Her poems appear or are forthcoming in many journals and anthologies, including *Blackbird, diode, North American Review, Prairie Schooner,* and *A Fierce Brightness: Twenty-Five Years of Women's Poetry*. She lives in Madison, Wisconsin. www.susanelbe.com.

Dina Elenbogen, an award-winning poet and prose writer, is the author of the poetry collection *Apples of the Earth* (2006). She has just completed a second poetry collection entitled *Aftermath*. Her poetry, essays, and stories have been widely published in magazines and anthologies. She has an M.F.A. in poetry from the Iowa Writer's Workshop and teaches at the University of Chicago Writer's Studio.

Martín Espada is the author of more than fifteen books. His latest collection of poems, *The Trouble Ball,* was released in 2011. His previous collection, *The Republic of Poetry* (2006), was a finalist for the Pulitzer Prize. The recipient of a Guggenheim fellowship, a USA Simon fellowship and the National Hispanic Cultural Center Literary Award, Espada is a professor of English at the University of Massachusetts–Amherst.

John W. Evans is a Jones Lecturer in poetry at Stanford University, where he was previously a Stegner Fellow. He is the author of the chapbooks, *No Season* (2011) and *Zugzwang* (2009). His poems appear in *Slate,* the *Missouri Review, Poetry Daily, Boston Review, Gettysburg Review,* the *Southern Review,* and elsewhere.

Beth Ann Fennelly directs the M.F.A. program at Ole Miss and lives in Oxford, Mississippi, with her husband and three children. She's won grants from the N.E.A., the Mississippi Arts Commission, and United States Artists. Fennelly has published three full-length poetry books and a book of nonfiction.

Michael Filimowicz is an interdisciplinary artist and an American Midwest transplant, currently residing in Vancouver, British Columbia, where he teaches at Simon Fraser University. The poem that appears in this anthology was written in a high-rise apartment in downtown Chicago.

Jennifer S. Flescher's poetry publications include the *Harvard Review, Fulcrum, Lit,* and the blog for the *Best American Poetry*. Her nonfiction publications include *AGNI Online, Jubilat,* the *Boston Globe,* and *Poetry Daily*. She holds an M.F.A. in poetry from Lesley University and an M.S.J. in journalism from Northwestern. She teaches writing and publishing to college students. She is editor and publisher of *Tuesday; An Art Project*.

Renny Golden's poetry book *Blood Desert: Witnesses 1820–1880* was published in December 2010. *Benedicite* was a White Pine Press finalist in 2010. She is a professor emerita from Northeastern Illinois University. Renny's poetry has appeared in *International Quarterly,* the *American Voice,* the *Literary Review, Americas Review,* and *The Book of Irish American Poetry: From the Eighteenth Century to the Present* (2007).

Linda Gregerson grew up in Cary, Illinois, forty miles from Chicago. Her books of poetry include *Magnetic North* (2007), *Waterborne* (2002), *The Woman Who Died in Her Sleep* (1996), and *Fire in the Conservatory* (1982). Her fifth book of poems, *The Selvage*, will be published in 2012.

John Guzlowski writes poems about his family's experiences in the Nazi concentration camps. His most recent books are *Lightning and Ashes* and *The Third Winter of War: Buchenwald*. He received the Illinois Arts Council Fellowship Award for poetry in 2001.

Terry Hamilton-Poore was born in Chicago and lived there until she was ten. Since then, she has lived in North Carolina, Missouri, Iowa, and California. Her poetry is informed by her geographical wanderings, as well as by her experiences as a wife, a mother, and a Presbyterian minister.

Joy Harjo is a poet, musician, performer, and playwright. *Soul Talk, Song Language*, a collection of interviews, columns, essays, and photographs, was published in 2011, and a memoir, *Crazy Brave*, is forthcoming. Her one-woman show "Wings of Night Sky, Wings of Morning Light" was accepted for production by the Public Theater in NYC, which is also commissioning her play, "I Think I Love You, an All Night Round Dance."

Derrick Harriell is working on a dissertation at the University of Wisconsin–Milwaukee, where he also teaches creative writing. A 2009 Pushcart nominee, Harriell has published poems in various literary journals and anthologies. *Cotton* is his first collection of poems.

Lola Haskins has published ten books of poems, most recently *The Grace to Leave* (2012), and two of nonfiction. Her poetry collection, *Still, the Mountain* (2010), won silver in the 2010 Florida Book Awards for poetry.

Bob Hicok's most recent book is *Words for Empty and Words for Full* (2010). A German translation of *This Clumsy Living* (2007) was released in 2011.

Edward Hirsch, who was born in Chicago, has published eight collections of poetry, most recently *The Living Fire: New and Selected Poems* (2010).

John Wesley Horton grew up in Valparaiso, Indiana. He has recently published poems in *Notre Dame Review, Malpais Review, Borderlands: Texas Poetry Review, Poetry Northwest*, and other magazines. He teaches writing and American literature in Seattle and codirects the University of Washington's summer creative writing program in Rome, Italy.

Randall Horton is the recipient of the Gwendolyn Brooks Poetry Award, the Bea González Prize for Poetry, and most recently a National Endowment for the Arts fellowship in literature. Horton is a Cave Canem fellow, a member of the Affrilachian Poets, and a member of the Symphony: The House That Etheridge Built. He is an assistant professor of English at the University of New Haven.

Ann Hudson's book, *The Armillary Sphere*, was selected by Mary Kinzie as the winner of the Hollis Summers Prize. Her work has appeared widely, including in *Crab Orchard Review*, the *North American Review, Orion, Poetry East, Prairie Schooner*, and the *Seattle Review*. She has lived in Chicago for more than a decade, though her roots to the city go back several generations. www.annhudson.net.

Donald Illich has published poetry in the *Iowa Review, LIT, Fourteen Hills, Passages North, Roanoke Review*, and *Cold Mountain Review*. He lives in Rockville, Maryland, where he works as a writer/editor for the government.

Larry Janowski's most recent book is *BrotherKeeper* (2007). He is a 2008 recipient of an Illinois Arts Council literary award and the winner of the 2010 Best Original Poem award by the Catholic Press Association. His work appears frequently in *After Hours: A Journal of Chicago Writing and Art*, as well as current or recent issues of *Rhino* and *Court Green*. Larry is a Franciscan friar and teaches at Loyola University.

Philip Jenks is the author of *On the Cave You Live In, My First Painting Will Be "The Accuser,"* and *Disappearing Address*, cowritten with Simone Muench. He is working on his fourth book, *Colony Collapse Metaphor* (2013) and teaches English at the University of Illinois at Chicago.

Thomas L. Johnson lives in Spartanburg, South Carolina, where he moved in 2002 after retiring as librarian emeritus from the University of South Carolina–Columbia. Tom has been winning awards as a poet, editor, and short fiction writer since the 1970s. A volume of his new and selected poems, *The Costume*, was published in 2010. He is a life member of the board of governors of the South Carolina Academy of Authors and was instrumental in editing the last literary map of the state.

Richard Jones is the author of seven books of poems, including *Apropos of Nothing, The Blessing*, and *The Correct Spelling & Exact Meaning*. Editor of the literary journal *Poetry East*, he is a professor of English at DePaul University in Chicago.

Jarret Keene is the author of the poetry collections *Monster Fashion* (2002) and *A Boy's Guide to Arson* (2009). He lives in Las Vegas, where his post-apocalyptical doom metal band Dead Neon terrorizes dive bars.

Susan Kelly-DeWitt is the author of *The Fortunate Islands* (2008), eight small press collections, and the electronic chapbook *The Limbo Suite*.

Becca Klaver is the author of the poetry collection *LA Liminal* (2010) and the chapbook *Inside a Red Corvette: A 90s Mix Tape* (2009). From 2005 to 2009 she lived in Chicago, where she received an M.F.A. in poetry from Columbia College Chicago (2007) and founded the feminist poetry press Switchback Books with Hanna Andrews and Brandi Homan (2006). Becca is currently a Ph.D. student in English at Rutgers University and lives in Brooklyn, New York.

Susanna Lang's first collection of poems, *Even Now,* was published in 2008, and she completed a second manuscript as a 2010 fellow at Hambidge. A chapbook, *Two by Two,* was published in 2011. Her poems have appeared in such journals as *New Letters, Little Star, Inkwell, Café Review,* the *Baltimore Review, Kalliope,* and *Green Mountains Review.* She lives in Chicago, where she teaches in the public schools.

Elizabeth Langemak's work has appeared in 32 *Poems,* the *Bellingham Review, Ninth Letter,* the *Cincinnati Review,* and *Best Poets: Fifty Poems by Emerging Writers.* She lives in Philadelphia, Pennsylvania.

Quraysh Ali Lansana is author of five poetry books and a children's book and is editor of eight anthologies. His most recent book is *Our Difficult Sunlight: A Guide to Poetry, Literacy, and Social Justice.* He is an associate professor of English/Creative Writing at Chicago State University.

Anna Leahy's collection *Constituents of Matter* won the Wick Poetry Prize. Her poems, essays, and stories have appeared in journals such as the *Southern Review, Fifth Wednesday,* the *Journal,* and *Crab Orchard Review,* and she cowrites Lofty Ambitions Blog. She edited the collection *Power and Identity in the Creative Writing Classroom* and teaches at Chapman University, where she directs Tabula Poetica.

Viola Lee graduated from New York University with a M.F.A. in poetry. Her recent poems have appeared in *Alice Blue, Pebble Lake Review, Caketrain,* and *Phoebe.* Her chapbook, *Another Word for Dialogue,* was a finalist with honorable mention in Kundiman's Vincent Chin Memorial Chapbook Competition. She lives in Chicago with her husband.

Brenna Lemieux has a bachelor's degree from Bucknell University and an M.F.A. from Southern Illinois University at Carbondale. She has lived in Maryland, Pennsylvania, France, and Ireland and currently lives and writes in southern Illinois.

Poet, translator, and filmmaker **Francesco Levato** is the author of three books of poetry: *Elegy for Dead Languages; War Rug,* a book length documentary poem; and *Marginal State.* He has translated into English the books of Italian poets Tiziano Fratus, *Creaturing,* and Fabiano Alborghetti, *The Opposite Shore.* His work has been published internationally in journals and anthologies, both in print and online, including *Drunken Boat,* the *Progressive, Versal,* and many others. His cinépoetry has been exhibited in galleries and featured at film festivals in Berlin, Chicago, New York, and elsewhere.

Gary Copeland Lilley is a North Carolina native who followed the blues from the Piedmont to Mississippi to Chicago. He earned his M.F.A. from Warren Wilson College. His publications include four collections of poetry, the most recent being *Alpha Zulu* (2008). He currently lives and teaches in Port Townsend, Washington.

Moira Linehan's debut collection, *If No Moon,* won the Crab Orchard Series in Poetry open competition and was published in 2007. Recent work has appeared or is forthcoming in *America,* the *Greensboro Review, Notre Dame Review, Poetry East, Salamander,* and *Wild Apples.* She lives in Winchester, Massachusetts.

Rachel Loden was born in Washington, DC, but grew up in Brooklyn, Berkeley, and Los Angeles. She is the author of *Hotel Imperium* and *Dick of the Dead* as well as four chapbooks, including *The Last Campaign* and *The Richard Nixon Snow Globe.* She received a fellowship from the California Arts Council, a grant from the Fund for Poetry, an &NOW award, and a Pushcart Prize. Her poems have also been included in two editions of *The Best American Poetry* and in *Western Wind: An Introduction to Poetry* (2005).

Marty McConnell cofounded the louderARTS Project (NYC) and founded and directs Vox Ferus (Chicago). Her publications include *Crab Orchard Review, Beloit Poetry Journal, Drunken Boat, Indiana Review, Salt Hill Review, Word Warriors: 35 Women Leaders in the Spoken Word Revolution,* and *Women.Period.* She appeared on two seasons of HBO's *Def Poetry Jam* and competed in seven National Poetry Slams.

Campbell McGrath is the author of nine books of poetry, most recently *In the Kingdom of the Sea Monkeys* (2012). A MacArthur and Guggenheim fellow, he lives in Miami and teaches at Florida International University, where he is the Philip and Patricia Frost Professor of Creative Writing.

Paul Martínez Pompa is the author of *Pepper Spray* (2006) and *My Kill Adore Him* (2009).

Adrian Matejka is the author of *The Devil's Garden.* His second book, *Mixology,* was a winner of the 2008 National Poetry Series and was nominated for a 2010 NAACP Image Award. "Jack Johnson Comes to Chicago" is from his forthcoming book *The Big Smoke: Jack Johnson Tells It.* He teaches at Southern Illinois University Edwardsville.

Erika Mikkalo lives and writes in Chicago. Her work received the Tobias Wolff Award for short fiction, and more recent writing has appeared in the *Beloit Poetry Journal, Ex-*

quisite Corpse, the2ndhand, *Massachusetts Review, Columbia Review, Fence, Another Chicago Magazine*, the *Chicago Review*, and other publications.

Wilda Morris is president of Poets and Patrons of Chicago and past president of the Illinois State Poetry Society. Her poems have appeared in the *Christian Science Monitor*, the *Alembic, Chaffin Journal*, and the *Kerf*. Her book, *Szechwan Shrimp and Fortune Cookies: Poems from a Chinese Restaurant*, was published in 2008. Her poetry blog is found at wildamorris.blogspot.com.

Simone Muench is the author of *The Air Lost in Breathing, Lampblack & Ash, Orange Crush*, and *Disappearing Address*, cowritten with Philip Jenks. She directs Lewis University's writing program, where she teaches creative writing and film studies. She is an editor for *Sharkforum*.

Julie Parson Nesbitt is author of the poetry collection *Finders*. She received the Gwendolyn Brooks Significant Illinois Poet Award and holds an M.F.A. in creative writing from the University of Pittsburgh. She served as executive director of the Guild Complex literary arts center and was director of development for Young Chicago Authors, which presents Louder Than a Bomb, the world's largest annual teen poetry festival.

Joey Nicoletti is the author of the poetry collections *Borrowed Dust* and *Cannoli Gangster*, which was selected as a finalist for the Steel Toe Books Poetry Prize by Denise Duhamel and is forthcoming in September 2012. A graduate of the M.F.A. program at Sarah Lawrence College, he currently teaches poetry writing and literature at Niagara University. www.joeynicoletti.com.

Barbra Nightingale's most recent books include *Two Voices, One Past* and *Geometry of Dreams*. She has had more than two hundred poems appearing in various literary journals and e-zines and is senior professor of English and creative writing at Broward College.

Raised in Michigan but now living in Southern California, **John F. Buckley and Martin Ott** began their ongoing games of poetic volleyball in the spring of 2009. Poetry from their collaboration has been accepted by the *Bryant Literary Review, Center, Compass Rose, Conceit Magazine, Eleven Eleven*, and *Splash of Red*. Their collaborative collection *Poets' Guide to America* will be published in 2012.

Elise Paschen is the author of *Bestiary, Infidelities*, winner of the Nicholas Roerich Poetry Prize, and *Houses: Coasts*. Former executive director of the Poetry Society of America, she is the editor of the *New York Times* best-selling anthology *Poetry Speaks to Children* and *Poetry Speaks Who I Am* and is coeditor of *Poetry Speaks* and *Poetry in Motion*, among other anthologies. Paschen teaches in the MFA Writing Program at the School of the Art Institute of Chicago.

Johanny Vázquez Paz was born in Puerto Rico. She published the book *Streetwise Poems/Poemas callejeros* (2007) and coedited the anthology *Between the Heart and the Land/Entre el corazón y la tierra: Latina Poets in the Midwest* (2001). She teaches at Harold Washington College in Chicago.

Todd James Pierce is the author of five books and anthologies, including *Newsworld* (2006), which won the Drue Heinz Literature Prize (selected by Joan Didion) and was a finalist for the John Gardner Book Award and the Paterson Prize. His work has been published in more than eighty magazines and journals, including the *Georgia Review*, the *Gettysburg Review*, *Indiana Review*, the *Iowa Review*, the *Missouri Review*, the *North American Review*, *Shenandoah*, the *Sun*, and *Willow Springs*. He codirects the creative writing program at California Polytechnic State University in San Luis Obispo, California.

James Plath grew up in Chicago's Portage Park neighborhood when there were still occasional horse-cart peddlers and a man who cruised the neighborhoods selling "RIPE FRESH STRAW-BERREES." James once caught an extra point at a Bears game played at Wrigley Field and survived a beating to keep the football. Some of his poems were collected in the chapbook *Courbet, on the Rocks*.

Chad Prevost is the author of several books and chapbooks. His work has recently been published in such places as the *Huffington Post, Hunger Mountain,* the *Seattle Review, Sentence,* and the *Southern Review*. He has just completed his debut novel, *The Director of Happiness*. Chad also serves as editorial director of C&R Press.

Mark Prudowsky works as an electrical contractor in western North Carolina. His writing has appeared in such journals as *Agenda, Lily, Wicked Alice, Cortland Review, Stolen River Review, Rivendell,* and *Wire Sandwich*.

Christina Pugh is the author of two books of poems: *Restoration* (2008) and *Rotary* (2004), which received the Word Press First Book Prize. The recent recipient of the Lucille Medwick Memorial Award from the Poetry Society of America and a fellowship in poetry from the Illinois Arts Council, she is an associate professor in the Program for Writers at the University of Illinois at Chicago.

Maya Quintero's poems have appeared in the *Atlanta Review, Flyway,* and *Phoebe*. She is currently working on a book-length poem based on the lives of 1940s Hollywood icons.

Robyn Schiff is the author of *Revolver* and *Worth*. She is an associate professor at the University of Iowa and coedits Canarium Books.

Teresa Scollon is the author of *To Embroider the Ground with Prayer*, forthcoming in 2012, and the chapbook *Friday Nights the Whole Town Goes to the Basketball Game*. She is a recent recipient of a fellowship from the National Endowment for the Arts and a past writer-in-residence at Interlochen Arts Academy. She lives in Traverse City, Michigan.

Don Share is senior editor of *Poetry* magazine. His books include *Squandermania, Union*, and *Seneca in English*. Forthcoming are a new book of poems, *Wishbone*, a critical edition of Basil Bunting's poems, and *Basil Bunting's Persia*. His translations of Miguel Hernández, collected in *I Have Lots of Heart*, were awarded the Times Literary Supplement Translation Prize. He has been poetry editor of *Harvard Review* and *Partisan Review*, editor of *Literary Imagination*, and curator of poetry at Harvard.

Vivian Shipley has published five chapbooks and nine books of poetry, most recently, *All of Your Messages Have Been Erased* (2010). She is a two-time recipient of the Paterson Award for Sustained Literary Achievement, and two of her books—*Gleanings: Old Poems, New Poems* and *When There Is No Shore*—were nominated for the Pulitzer Prize. Editor of the award-winning *Connecticut Review*, she is Connecticut State University Distinguished Professor at Southern Connecticut State University, where she was named Faculty Scholar in 2000, 2005, and 2008. Vivian lives in North Haven, Connecticut, with her husband, Ed Harris.

Barry Silesky has published four books of poetry, most recently *This Disease* (2009), and biographies of Lawrence Ferlinghetti and John Gardner. For thirty years he has lived in shadows of Wrigley Field with his wife, fiction writer Sharon Solwitz, and their son.

Patricia Smith is the author of six books of poetry, including *Blood Dazzler*, a finalist for the 2008 National Book Award, *Teahouse of the Almighty*, a National Poetry Series selection, and *Shoulda Been Jimi Savannah*. Her work has appeared in *Poetry*, the *Paris Review*, and *Best American Poetry 2011*. She is a professor at the CUNY/College of Staten Island and is on the faculty of Cave Canem and the Stonecoast M.F.A. program.

Dan Stryk's collections of poems and prose parables include *The Artist and the Crow* and *Solace of the Aging Mare*. A former N.E.A. poetry fellow and Illinois Arts Council poetry grant recipient, his work has appeared in *Poetry, Ploughshares, Antioch Review, New England Review*, and the *Oxford American*.

Lucien Stryk's numerous volumes of original poetry include *And Still Birds Sing: New & Collected Poems* and *Where We Are: Selected Poems*. He has been a lifelong supporter of regional arts, compiling two well-known anthologies of Midwestern poetry—*Heartland I* and its sequel, *Heartland II*—during his many years residing amid the farmlands of DeKalb, Illinois, just west of Chicago.

Onetime Chicago resident **Richard Terrill** is the author of two collections of poems, *Almost Dark* and *Coming Late to Rachmaninoff*, winner of the Minnesota Book Award, as well as two books of creative nonfiction, *Fakebook: Improvisations on a Journey Back to Jazz* and *Saturday Night in Baoding: A China Memoir*, winner of the Associated Writing Programs Award for nonfiction. He lives in Minneapolis.

Tony Trigilio's most recent book is the poetry collection *Historic Diary* (2011). He is a member of the core poetry faculty at Columbia College Chicago and is a cofounder and coeditor of *Court Green*.

Alpay Ulku's first collection, *Meteorology*, was published in 1999. His work has appeared in *Ploughshares, Boulevard, Witness, Epoch*, and the *Fiddlehead*. Alpay works as a business analyst in Chicago.

Judith Valente is an on-air correspondent for national PBS-TV. She is the author of the poetry collection *Discovering Moons* and the chapbook *Inventing an Alphabet*, selected by Mary Oliver for the 2005 Aldrich Poetry Prize, and is coeditor with Charles Reynard of *Twenty Poems to Nourish Your Soul*, an anthology of poems and reflections on finding the transcendent in the everyday.

N.E.A. Fellow **Martha Modena Vertreace-Doody** is Distinguished Professor of English and poet-in-residence at Kennedy-King College, Chicago, Illinois. *Glacier Fire*, her most recent book, won the Word Press Poetry Prize. Illinois Poet Laureate Kevin Stein published her poem "Walking under Night Sky" in his cassette "Bread & Steel: Illinois Poets Reading from Their Works."

Gale Renée Walden lives in Urbana, Illinois, but takes the train up to Chicago frequently. Moving to Chicago at the age of three, she doesn't feel as though she ever totally left. Chicago is, she has been known to explain to people not from there, the happiest city she has ever been in, but the joy is not frivolous. She has been teaching poetry in prisons.

Nicole Walker is the author of *This Noisy Egg* (2010). Her poetry and creative nonfiction have appeared in *Ploughshares*, the *North American Review, Bellingham Review, Fence*, the *Iowa Review, Fourth Genre, Ninth Letter*, and *Crazyhorse*, among other places. She has been awarded a fellowship from the National Endowment for the Arts and teaches at Northern Arizona University.

Ellen Wehle is a poetry reviewer and contributing editor at *West Branch*. Her first book, *The Ocean Liner's Wake*, came out in 2009. She lives in the Boston area with her husband and two dogs.

Scott Wiggerman is the author of two books of poetry, *Vegetables and Other Relationships* and *Presence*. Recent poems have appeared in *Switched-on Gutenberg, BorderSenses, Poemeleon, Broad River Review, Boxcar Poetry Review*, and *Southwestern American Literature*. A frequent workshop instructor, he is also an editor for Dos Gatos Press, publisher of the annual *Texas Poetry Calendar*, now in its fourteenth year, and publisher of *Wingbeats*, coedited by Wiggerman and David Meischen. http://swig.tripod.com.

Katherine Williams has authored three chapbooks and has read at venues throughout Southern California. She is published in various anthologies and has received a Push-cart nomination. She now lives on James Island with her husband, poet Richard Garcia, where she researches coral disease at Hollings Marine Lab.

Martin Willitts, Jr. was nominated for two Best of the Net awards and his fifth Push-cart award. He has four new chapbooks: *The Girl Who Sang Forth Horses* (2010), *Van Gogh's Sunflowers for Cezanne* (2010), *True Simplicity* (2011), and *My Heart Is Seven Wild Swans Lifting* (2011).

Janet Wondra's poetry is collected in three volumes, *Emerging Island Cultures*, *The Wandering Mother*, and *Long Division*. A new chapbook of poems, *Bad Attitude*, is forth-coming. Her work has also appeared in such journals as the *Southern Review*, *Witness*, *Michigan Quarterly Review*, *Connecticut Review*, and *Exquisite Corpse*. She teaches at Roosevelt University in Chicago.

A Florida native, **Stephen Caldwell Wright** is the founder and president of the Gwen-dolyn Brooks Writers Association of Florida. The author of several chapbooks and three poetry collections, *Making Symphony*, *Inheritance*, and *Perhaps on a Sunday Af-ternoon*, he has also been published in the *Carolina Quarterly*, *Florida Folktales*, *New Visions: Fiction by Florida Writers*, *Colorado Review*, *In Search of Color Everywhere*, *New Century North American Poets*, and *Beyond the Frontier: African-American Poetry for the 21st Century*.

Brenda Yates is from nowhere. After growing up on SAC bases here and overseas, she settled first in Massachusetts and then in California where she lives with her husband.

Permissions

Kathryn Almy, "Routes," appeared in *In Our Own Words: A Generation Defining Itself* Vol. 8. The poem appears here by permission of the author.

Nin Andrews, "At the Crawford Coal-Fired Power Plant," appears here by permission of the author.

Dori Appel, "Time Travel," appears by permission of the author.

Cristin O'Keefe Aptowicz, "Chicago Deep Dish," is reprinted from *Everything Is Everything* with permission from the author and Write Bloody Publishing.

Rane Arroyo, "Chicago's Monuments," appears by permission of the author.

Michael Austin, "Hancock O'Hare," appears by permission of the author.

Marvin Bell, "Yes, We Can," appeared in the *Iowa City Press-Citizen* on Jan. 20, 2009, and was later published as a broadside by Lost Horse Press. Copyright © 2009 by Marvin Bell. Reprinted by permission of the author.

Mary Grace Bertulfo, "Ted Stone Morning," appears by permission of the author.

Allen Braden, "Postcard from Buddy Guy's Legends: Bar and Grill, Chicago," appears by permission of the author.

John Bradley, "I Saw You," appears by permission of the author.

John F. Buckley and Martin Ott, "The Last Fortune Teller of Chicago," appeared in *Evergreen Review*, No. 122 (March 2010). Reprinted by permission of the author.

Melisa Cahnmann-Taylor, "Sixteen," appeared in a chapbook, *Reverse the Charges*. Reprinted by permission of the author.

Karen Carcia, "Everything Is," appears by permission of the author.

James E. Cherry, "Jean Baptiste," appears by permission of the author.

Susan Deer Cloud, "Sleeping with Carl," previously appeared in *Pitkin Review* (2009) and a chapbook, *Car Stealer* (Foothills Publishing, 2009). Reprinted by permission of the author.

James Conroy, "Hotel Dana," appears by permission of the author.

Timothy Cook, "Low Ride Elegy," appears by permission of the author.

Nina Corwin, "Campus Taxi," is from *The Uncertainty of Maps* by Nina Corwin. Copyright © 2011 by Nina Corwin. Reprinted by permission of CW Books and by permission of the author. The poem first appeared in *Atlanta Review*.

Curtis L. Crisler, "Michael Jordan," first appeared in *Dreamist: a mixed genre novel*. The poem appears here by permission of the author.

Mary Cross, "summer news," appears by permission of the author.

James D'Agostino, "Still Life with Zeno and File Footage," is from *Nude with Anything* (New Issues Press, 2006). Reprinted by permission of the author and by New Issues Press.

Stuart Dybek, "Ravenswood," first appeared in *Brute Neighbors* (DePaul Humanities Center). The poem appears here by permission of the author.

Bart Edelman, "Hibernation," is from *The Geographer's Wife*. Copyright © 2012 by Bart Edelman. Reprinted with the permission of Red Hen Press.

Susan Elbe, "Chicago Union Stockyards Circa 1957," first appeared in *MARGIE: The American Journal of Poetry*, Vol. 5 (2006). The poem appears here by permission of the author.

Dina Elenbogen, "150 Years of Chicago Architecture," first appeared in *Rhino* and was subsequently published in *Apples of the Earth* (Spuyten Duyvil, 2006). The poem appears here, with slight revisions, by permission of the author.

Martín Espada, "Cheo Saw an Angel on Division Street," is from *Rebellion Is the Circle of a Lover's Hands* (Curbstone, 1990). Copyright © 1990 by Martín Espada. Reprinted here, with slight revisions, by permission of the author.

John W. Evans, "Loop," appears by permission of the author.

Beth Ann Fennelly, "Asked for a Happy Memory of Her Father, She Recalls Wrigley Field," appeared in *Open House*, (W.W. Norton, 2009). The poem appears here by permission of the author.

Michael Filimowicz, "Radar Ghosts," appears by permission of the author. It originally appeared in *MARGIE*, No. 7 (Autumn 2008).

Jennifer S. Flescher, "With My Blue Flowered Dress," appeared in *Eclipse,* Vol. 18 (Fall 2007). The poem appears here by permission of the author.

Renny Golden, "Republic Steel Chicago South Works," first appeared in *Borderlands: Texas Poetry Review*, No. 17 (Winter 2001). The poem appears here by permission of the author.

Linda Gregerson, "The Horses Run Back to Their Stalls," first appeared in the *Atlantic* and subsequently in *Waterborne* (Mariner Books, 2004). Copyright © 2002 by Linda Gregerson. The poem appears here by permission of the author.

John Guzlowski, "38 Easy Steps to Carlyle's Everlasting Yea," appears by permission of the author.

Terry Hamilton-Poore, "Bible Belt," appears by permission of the author.

Joy Harjo, "The Woman Hanging from the Thirteenth Floor Window," appeared in *How We Became Human: New and Selected Poems* (W.W. Norton, 2002). The poem appears here by permission of the author.

Derrick Harriell, "Uncle Danny Brags about Playing Special Teams for the '85 Bears," first appeared in *Cotton* (Aquarius Press/Willow Books) and is reprinted here by permission of the author.

Lola Haskins, "Dearborn North Apartments," appears by permission of the author.

Bob Hicok, "In Michael Robins's class minus one," appeared in *This Clumsy Living*. Copyright © 2007 by Bob Hicok. Reprinted by permission of the University of Pittsburgh Press.

Edward Hirsch, "American Apocalypse," first appeared in *The Night Parade* (Alfred A. Knopf, 1989). The poem appears here by permission of the author.

John Wesley Horton, "Dear John Dillinger," originally appeared in *Here and There* (Fall 2006). The poem appears here by permission of the author.

Randall Horton, "on the other end. right there," appears by permission of the author.

Ann Hudson, "My Great-Grandfather Takes a Business Trip, c. 1912," appears by permission of the author.

Donald Illich, "Road Trip," appears by permission of the author.

Larry Janowski, "Luminaria," first appeared in *Rhino* (2001). The poem appears here, with slight revisions, by permission of the author.

Philip Jenks and Simone Muench, "Dear Chicago—," first appeared in *Disappearing Address*. Copyright © 2010 by Blaze Vox Books. The poem appears here by permission of the authors.

Thomas L. Johnson, "One likes to think Chicago," appears by permission of the author.

Richard Jones, "The Jewel," is reprinted from *The Correct Spelling & Exact Meaning* (Copper Canyon Press, 2010), Copyright © 2010 by Richard Jones. Reprinted by permission of the author.

Jarret Keene, "Chicago Noise (Love Letter to Steve Albini)," appears by permission of the author.

Susan Kelly-DeWitt, "Miniature Church," is reprinted from *Feather's Hand* (Swan Scythe Press, 2000). It appears here by permission of the author.

Becca Klaver, "Under the Terrible Burden of Destiny Laughing as a Young Man Laughs," appears by permission of the author.

Susanna Lang, "The Rainiest Day in Recorded Chicago History," appears by permission of the author.

Elizabeth Langemak, "At the Palmer House Hilton," first appeared in the *Cincinnati Review* 7.1 (2010). The poem appears here by permission of the author.

Quraysh Ali Lansana, "dead dead," appeared in *Sou'wester*, Vol. 38, No. 2. The poem appears here by permission of the author.

Anna Leahy, "At the Sea Lion Pool," appears by permission of the author.

Viola Lee, "Chicago: City of Neighborhoods," appears by permission of the author.

Brenna Lemieux, "Emerald Ash," appears by permission of the author.

Francesco Levato, "Seasonality of Violence," appears by permission of the author.

Gary Copeland Lilley, "Chicago Noir," was published in the collection *Alpha Zulu* (Ausable Press, 2008). The poem appears here by permission of the author.

Moira Linehan, "Too Much to Take In," appears by permission of the author.

Rachel Loden, "How Should Chicago Be Governed?," first appeared in *Boog City*. Copyright © 2010 by Rachel Loden. Reprinted by permission of the author.

Marty McConnell, "Fermata Chicago," appears by permission of the author.

Campbell McGrath, "Sandburg Variations," was previously published in *Knockout* and appears here by permission of the author.

Paul Martínez Pompa, "How to Hear Chicago," last appeared in *My Kill Adore Him* (University of Notre Dame Press, 2009). Reprinted by permission of the author.

Adrian Matejka, "Jack Johnson Comes to Chicago," appears by permission of the author.

Erika Mikkalo, "Chicago," appears by permission of the author.

Wilda Morris, "Noon outside the Music Mart: A Sestina," appears by permission of the author.

Judith Valente, "Run for Your Life," appeared in *Where We Live: Illinois Poets* (GreatUnpublished, 2003) and subsequently in *Discovering Moons: Poems* by Judith Valente. The poem appears here by permission of the author.

Martha Modena Vertreace-Doody, "Adagio Villanelle," appears by permission of the author.

Gale Renée Walden, "Nighthawks Transfixed," first appeared *Same Blue Chevy*, published by Northwestern University/Tia Chucha press. The poem appears here by permission of the author, with author's revisions.

Nicole Walker, "Inheritance," appears by permission of the author.

Ellen Wehle, "Cloud Gate," appeared in *Borderlands: Texas Poetry Review*. The poem appears here by permission of the author.

Scott Wiggerman, "The Facts as I Know Them," appears by permission of the author.

Katherine Williams, "Blueaille," appears by permission of the author.

Martin Willitts, Jr., "Fields," appears by permission of the author.

Janet Wondra, "At the Library," first appeared in *A Festschrift in Honor of Roosevelt University: Memories of the First 60 Years*. Reprinted by permission of the author.

Stephen Caldwell Wright, "Chicago Chronicle," appeared in *The Chicago Collective: Poems For and Inspired by Gwendolyn Brooks* (Christopherr-Burghardt: 1990). The poem appears here by permission of the author.

Brenda Yates, "Chicago," appears by permission of the author.

Index to Titles